A LEOPARD
TAMED

Kuac-Nyoat in Nasir (around 1960)

A LEOPARD TAMED

Eleanor Vandevort

HENDRICKSON
PUBLISHERS

A Leopard Tamed

Hendrickson Publishers Marketing, LLC
P. O. Box 3473
Peabody, Massachusetts 01961–3473

ISBN 978-1-68307-134-1

Unless otherwise noted, Scripture references are taken from the King James Version.

Drawings by James Howard

Originally published in 1968 by Harper & Row

Printed in the United States of America

First Printing 50th Anniversary Edition — February 2018

For more on the author's work among the Nuer, visit "Nuer Field Notes" archived at the IU Libraries African Studies Collection of the University at Indiana at http://www.dlib.indiana.edu/collections/nuer.

Library of Congress Cataloging-in-Publication Data

A catalog record for this title is available from the Library of Congress.
Hendrickson Publishers Marketing, LLC ISBN 978-1-68307-134-1

To

Arlene and Marian
Bob and Vi
My colleagues at Nasir—
nurse, teacher, doctor, and his faithful wife

They, too, felt the heat and the rain
  Killed the snakes
  Answered a thousand requests
  Battled with the language
  Gave away razor blades, nails, and safety pins
    buttons, thread, and old tin cans
  Taught the youngest ones and the oldest ones how to read

  Answered the midnight calls of
    Doctor, Come—I was eaten by a scorpion, and
    Doctor, Come—my wife is giving birth

And they, too, felt the pain of the people
    and waited and prayed
    rejoiced and were discouraged—and finally, evicted
But are still believing, waiting for the early and the latter rains
  Waiting for the harvest

For the Lord of hosts hath purposed, and who shall disannul
it? And his hand is stretched out, and who shall turn it back?
                    (Isaiah 14:27)

CONTENTS

FOREWORD

It was the severest test of faith I knew: to believe Him, not for what he would do, for that is only one infinitesimal aspect of God, but for who He is. . . . Now as I left, I knew for myself, at least, that God meant what He had said: that I was to know, to understand God is God, and leave His defense up to Him.

—Eleanor Vandevort

You have in your hands a mysterious story, crafted by a master storyteller—a woman who was herself a study in mystery and paradox. Eleanor Vandevort was a woman of profound Christian faith, certain of Jesus Christ and yet ready to question everything else. She was a farm girl from Pennsylvania who set out on a freighter to Sudan, Africa, having never been more than a few hundred miles from the home in which she grew up. As a single white woman, she entered into the naked blue-black tribe of the Nuer, where her life without a husband and a child was as strange to them as their lives were to her, and yet they came to call her *Nyarial, e ram anath*—"a person of the people." She lived most of her life under the belief that her work in the Sudan had produced nothing for the kingdom of Christ, only to discover, in the last decade of her life, that the children of her Nuer friends had escaped the Sudanese genocide, had found their way to America, and revered her as the one in whose legacy they lived as faithful followers of Jesus.

This is a woman and a story you want to know. It just might change your life. It certainly changed mine.

When I first met Eleanor Vandevort—or Van, as she was known to me—Africa was far behind her. She had moved on to a new "tribe," the students at Gordon College. She labored in an obscure office in the basement of the student center. She taught the Bible in her home. She almost never spoke of her time in the Sudan, the friends she had left behind, the mysteries that remained unsolved.

For my part, I was in a kind of crisis, having just come to seminary after working as a counselor to pastors and their families. I was awash in things I could not explain; put at odds within myself by the contradictions of human nature, the very fallible church, and the inadequacy of all answers proffered by well-meaning Christians up to that point in my life. The religious language that seemed to come so easily to so many was of no comfort to me, and I often felt alone with my questions and my turmoil.

I was lost. But in Van I found the great champion of questions and mysteries. She was not afraid! Africa had cured her of that. I found solace in her oft-heard refrain, "What does it *mean?*" She was willing to question everything. And for her, hard questions were the pathway to well-tested faith.

Van took my questions, and my fears, and led me in the way of Christ. She became my dearest friend. We often traveled together, we built her retirement home together—and then *re*built it when the first house burned in a fire. Finally, I cared for her when she could no longer live alone. We talked together every day and worked at the questions of faith every day. On her last day on earth, we sat together until her last breath took her into the arms of Jesus.

I know of what I speak when I tell you the person you meet and walk with until the last page of *A Leopard Tamed* lived beyond the end of this story and into a whole lifetime of praise to the God who took her to Africa. In this she taught me, and so very many others, that great mysteries can lead to great certainties—not certainties of outcomes, but certainties about the character of God. To the very end she said, "Do not be afraid. The Lord is with us!" By that she meant, do not be afraid of questions, do not be afraid of the unexplained, do not be afraid of death, do not be afraid when you walk in dark places, do not be afraid to tell the truth. God is faithful. For Van, that was the rock that would never move.

When *A Leopard Tamed* was first published in 1968, this honest account of missions was not well received. Van was so very far ahead of her time in understanding the cultural endangerments and theological quandaries embedded in the then-accepted methods of missions, and yet she believed thoroughly in Jesus' command to go into all the world. At the time of its original writing, the world of evangelical missions did not yet have a framework that could hold those two things in tension.

Now, fifty years later, *A Leopard Tamed* is returned to us in this special 50th anniversary edition, and perhaps we may be better able to receive its message. Authenticity is a premium value for our modern age, and *A Leopard Tamed* delivers it. This reprint is a testament both to its penetrating writing and its prophetic account of what authentic Christian witness ought to look like.

Several people should be mentioned for making possible this new edition of *A Leopard Tamed*. It was Carrie Martin, one of Van's dear friends and a caregiver in the latter years of her life, who brought the original book to the attention of Hendrickson Publishers and convinced them of its relevance for today's reader. This new edition of the book is further enriched and brought full circle in a lovely way by Valerie Elliot Shepard, who has added a new introduction as a companion to the one her mother, Elisabeth Elliot, provided fifty years ago. Finally, many thanks are due to the editorial staff at Hendrickson Publishers and to Patricia Anders in particular. They have seen the depth and value of this work and made it possible for a new generation of Christians to be trained and nourished by it.

Of course, Van was not alone on the mission field at Nasir, Sudan, and she dedicates *A Leopard Tamed* to her co-laborers in the gospel. The "mission nurse," as Van calls her in the book, is her very dear friend Arlene Schuiteman, a pioneer in the training of nurses on the mission field. Arlene's story is told in Jeff Barker's book *Sioux Center Sudan: A Farm Girl's Missionary Journey* (Hendrickson, 2018).

*Arlene Schuiteman (left) and Eleanor Vandevort (right)
in Nasir (around 1958)*

Before sending you on to discover this treasure, I offer one last thought. It is perhaps abundantly clear by now that if you are looking for a book that sets human events in their most cheerful light, then this is not the book for you. Put it down and back away slowly! But if you have come up against life and are looking for the way through, if you are looking for a story that reveals a path of faith in the midst of paradox and mystery—then, by all means, read on in earnest.

Trudy Summers
Global Honors Institute
Gordon College
Wenham, Massachusetts

INTRODUCTION TO THE 50th ANNIVERSARY EDITION

I am deeply privileged to be asked to write this new introduction for my "Dear Aunt Van's" book (although she was no relation to me, I called her "aunt" because most missionary children call adults on the field "aunt" and "uncle"). In 2015, she was promoted to the place of glory, where we shall see Jesus as he is and we shall be made like him. She died the same year as my mother, Elisabeth Elliot, following my mother only four months later. I've never known anyone besides my mother who truly longed for heaven as she did in her many years of being an invalid. She called herself "Oh Aunt Van" to me, because I often said that to her when she'd make me laugh, and sometimes when I was frustrated with her. She called me "Tiny Teenser," which was her affectionate and playful nickname for me, as well as "Baleria" (what the Quichua Indians called me). In 1962, Aunt Van came to live with us in the Amazon jungle, and then in 1963 she came to Franconia, New Hampshire, when we moved there, staying with us until my mother remarried in 1969.

As Aunt Van talked with her about her experience in the Sudan, my mother strongly urged her to write her intriguing missionary story. They had become best friends in gym class at Wheaton College, not just because they were both quite nonathletic, but also because they enjoyed studying Greek and passionately loved God. They both wanted to be missionaries and hoped to be able to translate the New Testament into a foreign language—whatever language God called them as missionaries to work in. My mother's book, *These Strange Ashes*, has a similar conclusion to *A Leopard Tamed*, which I won't spoil for you if you are reading this story for the first time!

I remember Aunt Van sitting at my grandparents' antique desk in Franconia with a small typewriter, struggling with the writing and complaining about her inability to write well. I know they both had read and continued to devour any work by Isak Dinesen—the Danish coffee farmer and author who wrote *Out of Africa* with beautiful descriptions and stories of her life there. Unfortunately, I was too young to sympathize or be too concerned over what Aunt Van was writing—and then I became too busy as a teen to read it, even at an age when I would have appreciated it. Then, in 2013 or 2014, when I visited her in Gloucester, Massachusetts, where she spent the last eight years of her life, I finally asked her about it.

How often she made me laugh with her sense of fun and hilarity, along with my mother's. She helped me enjoy life and appreciate what God has given us. She also had a beautiful singing voice and could harmonize on any piece, by ear. On Saturday afternoons, she played operatic pieces, either as recordings or on the radio while we cleaned the house, which made me love soprano voices.

I have now read *A Leopard Tamed* with delight, fascination, and complete empathy, as I know the same agonies of mission work my mother and father endured in Ecuador. To me, Aunt Van's writing is impeccable, and I know you will appreciate her daily keen observations, depth of understanding of the human heart, and her serious and often intense view of what it means to follow Christ.

When I was a young girl, I thought she was too serious at times, and I was afraid she judged me because I was so full of play and laughter. As I grew, however, I realized it was not judgment of my character but a sincere desire to help me to understand what my mother and father had committed their lives to, and to question my commitments as I entered the adolescent years, when I was so easily swayed by friends and current trends.

This story of the barren, hot, and dry southern Sudan, and the inexplicable ways of the Nuer tribesmen, along with her sharp-edged observations of their thinking, has made me laugh and cry.

The descriptions of the climate, the natural environment, and the views she had of this (to us readers) inhospitable country are vivid. I remember "connecting" with her in her love of nature (I *loved* being outdoors) and her acute reflections on what God had created for us.

This book is "good talk" as the Nuer would say, which means it is true and to be listened to. The thinking of these primitive people was as old as creation, and sometimes Aunt Van was completely puzzled by their lack of logic, planning, or inability to learn simpler and more efficient ways of doing things. But then she pondered their absolute contentment in all situations. They accepted death as part of life's or God's way of punishment, thinking that the only way to appease him was to sacrifice an ox. Although they did not seek to avoid death, they began to want and need the white man's "magic" (the medicines of the nurses or doctors). If it didn't work, however, then they were sure it was because someone in the family had done wrong and, unfortunately, that the white man's talk was "not good." And if they couldn't figure out why something bad happened, they would say God was punishing them and simply accepted it without much attempt to "figure things out," as the white man does. They had no science, and therefore their rationale for death was simply because God was angry. God was both the God of death as well as the God of life. They had no understanding of a God of love, until some of them began to accept the truths of the gospel—or "God's talk."

One young mother brought her daughter, who she thought was dying, to the clinic. When a nurse spoke to the mother about her daughter getting well, her thoughts went thus:

> My heart was glad to hear this. It is the plan of God, I think. I heard a man talking about God while I was sitting under the tree. He said God gives people life. That is good. That is what I want for Nyaliaa. I am happy that I came to the house of magic.

In my mother's original introduction, she wrote,

> I feel as though I have [traveled and seen the Nuer] now that I
> have read *A Leopard Tamed*. For here is an inside story. Here
> is a long, deep, careful look at a people—and at one of them
> in particular, Kuac, the "Leopard" of the title—given us by a
> woman who, as long as I have known her, has wanted above
> everything else to *know* people, to understand them and to
> learn who and why they are. The first time I saw her . . . [she
> had] in her hand a tiny New Testament which she was reading,
> trying to find out for herself what God was like, who His Son
> Jesus was, and what He had to say to her. She has never given
> up this quest during thirteen years with the Nuer.

Aunt Van's learning from these remarkable people gave her genuine love and concern for them. She never says this in these pages,
but the reader senses her commitment to them, even though they
can hardly understand her ways, nor she theirs. She speaks simply
and straightforwardly to them, especially to Kuac. He respected her
and she respected him, "listening well" and answering him always
in complete honesty. God had given her a young man to whom,
as he taught her Nuer, she could first teach English and then the
truths of the Bible. He was intelligent and hungry to learn. In turn,
he taught her the thinking of their people, their taboos, and their
traditions. He was a man who knew later that he was called of God
to speak "God's talk" earnestly and clearly to his people, and she
saw him as her greatest friend and helper.

When they began translating Scripture stories into the Nuer
language, there were many difficulties, as the language didn't have
words for many of our English words for spiritual truths. In *A Leopard Tamed*, Aunt Van didn't write of only his success or her success with him. She also relates the pitfalls of his wanting to learn
Western ways, his struggle to obey Scripture when other Christians
from the "official mission board" were telling him what to do, and
when it was too difficult to follow.

Aunt Van's faith was in a mysterious but always perfect God. She couldn't answer all of the Nuers' questions, but she loved them enough to be honest that God would always do right, even when we did not expect or want a particular outcome. I end with a C. S. Lewis quote from *Mere Christianity*, because no one could have said it better:

> [To have faith in Christ] means, of course, trying to do all that He says. There would be no sense in saying you trusted a person if you would not take his advice. Thus, if you have really handed yourself over to Him, it must follow that you are trying to obey Him. But trying in a new way, a less worried way. Not doing these things in order to be saved, but because He has begun to save you already. Not hoping to get to Heaven as a reward for your actions, but inevitably wanting to act in a certain way because a first faint gleam of Heaven is already inside you.

To me, there was a "strong" gleam of heaven in Aunt Van, and I am thankful for her life of love, joy, and serious obedience to his call on her. Her respect of this primitive tribe, so different from the typical Westerners' reaction to them, was what helped them to love her. She gave the Truth to many Nuer with love. Some accepted it and believed, while others did not. Although they wondered at her different culture and odd ways, they had a candid, unguarded confidence in her—and through her presence and her love, Aunt Van helped them see that "gleam of Heaven."

Valerie Elliot Shepard
Southport, North Carolina

*Eleanor Vandevort, Valerie Elliot, and Elisabeth
Elliot in Franconia, New Hamphsire (1966)*

*Eleanor Vandevort, Elisabeth Elliot, and Valerie
Elliot in Franconia, New Hamphsire (1966)*

INTRODUCTION TO THE ORIGINAL EDITION

Elisabeth Elliot

Nasir, a little town in the south Sudan on the bank of the Sobat River, was a place you could hardly get to, and very few people ever wanted to. If you did get there, there was hardly any place to go. You might go northwest a hundred and sixty miles to the town of Malakal, or southeast about thirty miles to the border of Ethiopia—by river, if it was the rainy season, or by road if it was the dry. There *was* a road—the only road anywhere around that had been made by white men, and like most white men's roads, it was as straight as they could make it, hacking through the tough clumps of grass called sudd, building up the low places with mud on mud (for the country had no stones at all). At best it was a double-wheel track, unbelievably rough and pitted and treacherous, but it was straight. Down the center, between the two ruts made by the white man's wheels, ran the Nuer trail. Nuers walked, and where they walked they made trails. None of the trails was straight—why should they be straight? And so this one, tramped out after the foreigners had made their wheel-trail, jerked and jutted and turned crazily between the straight lines. It did not occur to the Nuer that there was any reason to follow the track of the wheel. It did not seem to him easier or more logical or better in any way. He was not looking for easier or more logical or better ways of doing the things he knew well how to do and had been doing since time out of mind. It was the white man who was always searching, never satisfied, always wanting change.

Into the land of the Nuer, the Sudan's Upper Nile Province, the white man has come, but it has never been for long, and the impression he has made has not been deep. The land does not welcome him—it is a dry, incredibly flat, hard-baked land of few natural beauties and many hardships. The white man has found other parts of Africa far more inviting. But he has, on occasion, had reason to enter the Nuer's country—Britain governed the area jointly with Egypt, and officials were stationed in isolated places, usually for short periods; other white men explored the great river, the Nile, in order to find its source; to the only two towns of the south Sudan, Juba and Malakal, Greek merchants and one or two Indians have gone to establish businesses. Otherwise, few have been drawn to the barren grasslands. Of these few, some are missionaries, who believe in values other than material and political. They have all left their marks—there are some buildings, some laws and systems, some pith helmets and khaki shorts which other white men find familiar, but for the most part the African people who belong here are as they have always been. The white man's track runs as he wanted it to, and the black man's runs his way.

"Look," says the white man. "Walk here. This is the way. It is smooth and straight and easy. Your way is crooked and hard."

And the Nuer stands on one foot, his arm crooked around his fishing spear, his chin held high. He looks away, past the foreigner, across the slow, thick, snaking river to the sweeping plain. He has no landmarks other than these—the river and the plain—but he knows where he is, he belongs here in the land, and he knows the way that he takes.

I am not one of those who has ever found his way to Nasir. I have never seen a Nuer. But I feel as though I have done both now that I have read *A Leopard Tamed*. For here is an inside story. Here is a long, deep, careful look at a people—and at one of them in particular, Kuac, the "Leopard" of the title—given us by a woman who, as long as I have known her, has wanted above everything else to *know* people, to understand them, and to learn who and why they are. The first time I saw her, she was sitting on the floor of a college gymnasium waiting for the class to begin. She wore a blue gym suit, and her long legs were stretched out on the floor in front of her. In her hand was a tiny New Testament which she was reading, trying to find out for herself what God was like, who His Son Jesus was, and what He had to say to her.

She has never given up this quest, and during thirteen years with the Nuer people she learned from them as she lived with them and loved them. She has shown them to us here, from the strange and somewhat frightening initiation of young men to the death of old Yuol who had traveled in the sky canoe and who understood that God wants us to be His "praisers." She has shown us Kuac, the young schoolboy so unusual in his perception and abilities, who went to school and seminary and became the first and only Nuer pastor and her own right-hand man in the task of Bible translation. She has not been satisfied to show us only his successes, but has probed deeply and often painfully into the problems that confronted him in his desire to serve God rather than mammon, in the pressures brought to bear upon him by his unique responsibilities to fellow tribesmen and at the same time to alien overseers of the church. We see him in his relation to his people with their polygamy, their blood sacrifice, their taboos and customs and legends; in his relation to the missionaries, with their sometimes too easy solutions to problems they did not fully understand; in his relation to the God he had learned to trust and was trying to lead his people to trust. And we see it all through the eyes of one who observed (she shows us the baked earth of the land, the flocks of crows like "aerial bishops," the white merciless sunlight, the huddled huts on the shimmering plain), who sympathized (she helps us to understand as she herself understood why the Nuers did what they did), and who, above all, loved them and wanted to share with them everything she had.

She found to her dismay that this sharing was not so simple as she had anticipated. The Nuer trail ran still crooked between the straight lines laid down. The heart of the people seemed often closed—not alone by their will or her incompetence. There remained for her and for Kuac questions which seemed to have no answers, but it was this very fact that gave them room for faith. Gerhard Ebeling writes, in *The Nature of Faith,* "It would be folly to say that faith's sphere is where one sees nothing. Rather, its sphere is where one sees a great deal, so terribly much that one involuntarily closes one's eyes, because the sight is unendurable. But faith does not believe because it closes its eyes. Rather, faith means to hold and trust, with eyes that see, to what one does not see; to hope against hope, to believe against experience."

This was the task set for the author—the missionary—and for Kuac. And when, in the end, Kuac found himself shut up in prison, his prayer was, "Make me all that I can be in Jesus."

There is, I believe, a great hunger today for truthfulness, for "the straight story." Missionary books have at times portrayed victories out of all proportion to the difficulties and defeats. But this is not a help to faith. It is, if we can accept Ebeling's definition, rather a hindrance. This book, however, may help us to see a great deal, some of it nearly unendurable, and if we can look courageously we may perhaps be enabled to believe in the God who has taken to Himself the whole responsibility for the ultimate answers.

NOTE ON PRONUNCIATION
OF NUER WORDS

The Nuer language is written phonetically. However, to facilitate an easier pronunciation, much of the spelling in this book has been Anglicized. But *c*, as it appears, is pronounced *ch*, and *a* before *c* is pronounced long *i*. For example, Kuac's name is pronounced *Kw-i-ch*, long i (like *quite* but with a *ch* instead of a *t*).

Eleanor Vandevort and Kuac Nyoat with fellow
Nuer man in Nasir (around 1952)

1

A NUER BOY COMES OF AGE

"Please, Nyarial," Kuac said, calling me by the tribal name I'd been given, "remember, when the airplane comes, I want kerosene. My kerosene is finished and my lamp has no kerosene. The airplane will bring it."

"All right, Kuac," I said, "we'll see. I will write a letter. Perhaps the airplane can bring it."

He turned and walked away, out of my gate and along the river. He was the pastor of the mission church, one of the most educated and advanced men of his tribe—the Nuer—one of whom the mission was justly proud and proof that in the south Sudan Africans were on the move. Still, a visible vestige of his past remained. You could not miss it in spite of his white robe or how well he preached. It was the mark of his initiation into manhood—those six horizontal lines cut in parallel rows across his forehead from ear to ear.

When I first came to Africa I thought of this rite as a mark of heathenism pure and simple, but then, as time passed, I began to wonder how adequate my judgment was.

It was ten years after my arrival in Africa that I actually saw the initiation rite take place. It was in December. The rains were over, the ground was dry. The grain had been harvested, and the thick stocks cut down and made into fences around the courtyards. The wind now blew from the north, cooling the atmosphere. Man Gaac, a Nuer woman and a Christian with three grown children, came to me and said, "Ruey will be given his marks tomorrow. Shall we not go together?"

I was surprised and delighted that she would ask me. I had never seen this done before. I had never been invited. Ruey was her second youngest son, in his mid-teens. Yes, I wanted to go, I said, asking, "What time will you come?"

"Very early in the morning, before the bell is rung," she said. She meant the workmen's bell at the United Presbyterian mission which was rung each weekday at six o'clock.

The next day Man Gaac was at the door clapping for me, before the sun was in the sky, and before anyone was on the path. Across the river—which was level with the bank, as smooth as glass, and mirrored a flock of white egrets that skimmed its dark-green surface in rapid flight on their way to the feeding ground—the weaverbirds in the bamboo grove were stirring and filling the air with their frenetic chirping. It was the time of day when one could almost believe there was no trouble or sorrow in the world. Man Gaac was wearing a white dress—a recent missionary discard—and a pair of rundown nursing shoes.

"Did you eat?" she asked me after the greetings were exchanged.

"No, I did not eat."

"Hunger will kill you," she said, knowing our custom of an early breakfast.

"No, I will live, old mother, it will not kill me," I replied. She did not sit down. She was eager to be on the way in order to arrive in time before the cutter had begun his work.

We left the house and with our backs to the river, went past the school compound, past the army's quarters, across the clay road and out toward the village. It was not far to our destination, but we walked with a quick pace, our shoes clomping on the hard footpath, ahead of the sun, and our faces to the wind. Brown, skeletal weeds rolled weightlessly over the ground with every gust. Thick stubble now marked where the grain had been, and termites' tunnels encrusted the dried-out rubble.

In a short time we could look back and see the lone, green strip of land bordering the Sobat River, which marked the government-mission settlement of Nasir.

The world was an enormous circular stage and wherever you walked or stood on it, you felt yourself to be always in the center with nothing between you and the far horizon.

Man Gaac was ahead, loping easily, her head held high like a giraffe. We passed the thorn tree beyond which the path forked, and followed to the right. The morning light was strong. The sun came up quickly, sat for a moment like an orange plate on the rim of the earth, then lifted into the pale sky, sending out a sudden heat, warming my back. Man Gaac had not spoken since we started out. She was preoccupied with her thoughts. "Old mother," I said, "will the marking be done at your place?"

She did not hear me in the rush of the wind. I asked again.

"No," she answered, not stopping or slackening her pace.

The village behind the government post was very large. It was called Kuanylualthoaan because a man by the name of Lual *picked up* (kuany) *a wild cat* (thoaan) there. The section of the village where Man Gaac lived was called "the center of the village." It was a unit of mud huts and barns strung out in uneven fashion all by itself. As we walked through it, only the cattle were awake to watch us go by. Everything was golden in the long rays of the sun—the cattle, their curved horns, the ash-dust they slept in, the huts and barns enclosed in their fences. One straggly sesaban tree growing by the cornstalk fence distinguished Man Gaac's place from everyone else's. We came up to it and went in.

The clay yard had been swept clean. An old lady sat against the hut with her legs stretched out in front of her, trying to light a long-stemmed pipe. Man Gaac left me standing there and crawled into the hut. I greeted the old woman. "Are you at peace, old mother?"

"*Uh*," she said, meaning yes, "I am at peace." She spoke automatically and as fast as possible so as not to stop the sucking rhythm needed to fire the coals in the clay-pipe bowl which was at the end of the two-foot wooden stem on the ground.

Man Gaac came out and said to the woman, "Did Gat-kuoth come?"

"*Uh,* he is in the barn," the old woman answered, bending over her pipe.

"Let us go," Man Gaac said to me.

The mud barn was just outside the fence. Gatkuoth was stand-ing in front of it as we came out of the yard. He was Man Gaac's second-eldest son. He was tall and heavier than most Nuer men, and he wore a very large ivory bracelet around his arm, and red beads at his waist, and nothing else.

"Have the boys gone?" Man Gaac asked him.

"*Uh,* they have already gone," he said. Then he greeted me. "It is you, Nyarial?" he said. "You have come for the marking?"

"*Uh,* I have come for the marking."

"We will go," said Man Gaac.

"Go," he said, and we turned and went on through the village.

We headed toward the river again. The sun was in front of us now and rising slowly. The softness of the dawn was gone, but the air was cool. This was the best time of the year for the marking, when the air had some freshness in it and there would be fewer flies.

It must be a gory business, I thought to myself, recalling a story I had heard about a white man who had watched an initia-tion and fainted. I can't imagine fainting. I can't even imagine feel-ing sick. I would have once, but living here has changed me. When I first came there was that little girl they fished out of the river at Christmastime—how her body stank, and the sight of it, bloated and pink; I couldn't get it out of my mind for days. I could smell it and smell it and smell it. But last year, that other little girl—I fished her out myself and it didn't bother me at all. It's a good thing I've changed, otherwise I never would have made it. That man con-vulsed with tetanus. That beautiful young woman on the table, in-ternal hemorrhage, no hope, her baby dead, and that old mother on the floor, clutching her head in her hands. You've got to change. Those Siamese twins—the man threw them out on the ground for me to see—what a man, but I looked at them, that's the thing. He didn't care, so I didn't care. How can you care? Life is too stark to care too much. Reet didn't care. He levered out his little boy's six lower teeth just as everyone else does—clunk, clunk, clunk, clunk, clunk, clunk—and they were gone. And Reet's a believer. But it's the way of the people. Do you want to look like a hyena? That's what they say. Who is to argue that one?

As I was wondering if we were never going to get there (not that we had walked very far, but just that I was becoming impatient), Man Gaac stopped beside a hut with a fence around it as if she had come upon the scene of an accident. A man sitting against the fence, warming himself in the morning sun, looked at us but did not speak. He wore only bracelets and beads like Gatkuoth, but his body was completely covered in gray ashes. All around him the ground was flat and bare. There was no grass and no trees—nothing between him and the mud barn ahead. A small group of men stood by the barn, but none of them spoke to us. It was a unique occasion. Everywhere people always greeted me, but not today. Man Gaac said nothing, so neither did I.

Outside the barn, under the open sky, three boys were stretched out side by side on the ground. Ruey, Man Gaac's son, was in the middle lying with his head tilted back and neatly cushioned in a pile of dung ash, his eyes at dead center and still, his arms folded across his bare chest, his feet crossed at the ankles. His body was void of all ornaments, his head was shaved, and the soles of his feet faced the dark, oval opening of the mud barn.

In back of where the boys were lying, a few yards away, the cattle were tied, each animal to its tethering post (a short stick pounded into the ground with a wooden mallet), and blue wisps of smoke drifted upward from the smoldering dung fires laid down there the night before. Behind the cattle was the plain with clusters of huts and barns standing in drab blotches of grays and faded yellow. Behind the huts and barns was the scrub forest, etched in black on the horizon.

The sun was beginning to burn now as it climbed into the sky, and the flat, black shadows it had laid down were shortening and fading away.

I would have done this inside the fence, I thought to myself, where it's more private. But inside the fence by the hut was women's ground, and today these boys were leaving their mothers and becoming men. Where we were standing was men's ground, a place reserved for men and cattle.

A man came out of the barn, followed by two other men. Ducking his head out from under his cloth, the first man took off the cloth, baring himself, and threw it onto the thatch. He came over to where the boys lay, wearing only beads at his waist, an ivory bracelet on his arm, and a large, yellow plastic comb in his hair. He had a crude piece of sharp metal in his hand. The boys were as three smooth saplings, stripped of their leaves— "emptied," as the people spoke of anyone whose decorations had been removed.

Everyone gathered around as the cutter knelt down. Man Gaac stood behind Ruey; I was at his feet. No one spoke. The ground was hard, and I wondered that the boys never moved, that the black biting ants did not bother them, stinging the soft skin under their legs.

The cutter began on the right side of the boy to my right. This was as it had to be. The reverse would have been impossible. The right side indicated manliness, goodness, and strength. The left indicated femininity, evil, and weakness. He placed the knife in the middle of the boy's forehead just above the eyebrows, then with his left hand he turned the boy's face as he cut a thin red line across that side of the forehead to behind the right ear. He repeated this, cutting lines one above the other, the second time, the third time, the fourth, fifth, and sixth times—which was the end of the right side.

Then he crawled around to the boy's left side and began again, his thick toes supporting him against the hard ground as he bent over, this time holding the top of the boy's head with his left hand, twisting it away from him as he pulled the knife over the soft, black-velvet skin. The blood oozed freely now, trickling out of the rutted skin, making tiny streams, running down the forehead and behind both ears where it began to coagulate and to drop heavily into the ashes.

The difficulty of the cutter's job was intensified as his field of operation became loose and sticky. But he was aided by the motionless attitude of the boy who, appearing to be numb to the pain, yielded his head to the man's control. Crooked cuts meant crooked scars to remain on permanent display, a testimony to the fact that the boy had flinched. The cutter worked quickly, drawing his knife over the forehead as one would draw with a pencil, only pressing it forcefully into the skull. He finished. The boy's forehead was now a gleaming scarlet, seeping up and flowing slowly in rivulets to the ground.

A second man knelt down behind the boy to shoo the flies from his face. He did this, I imagined, not for hygienic reasons, but to prevent any irritation.

The cutter was now on his feet and turned to Ruey, who appeared to be the youngest of the three. As resolute as the first boy, he remained stock-still when the cutter put the knife to his head. It made a difference in my attitude toward this initiation that I knew Ruey and his family, and that his mother had asked me to come. I had a reason for being there and for trying to appreciate what was going on. It was surprisingly difficult, but as I watched Ruey, I found my spirit cheering him on, eager that he get through the ordeal as well as the first boy. This made me think back over his life as you might do when attending someone's graduation. Ruey had grown up with the boys in his village, tending the sheep and goats, cleaning out the barns each morning, and setting the dung fires for the cattle at night. His goal as a boy was to become a man. Now that day was here. He had been drawn to it as metal to a magnet. He had no alternative, and wanted none. It was his graduation day, the greatest day in his life. He was becoming a man!

I thought back to my earliest days in the Sudan, to my introduction to the initiation rite, and my preconceived ideas. It had happened at night, shortly after my arrival at the mission. The nurse answered a call from the village to come see a man who was bleeding, and I went with her. In the hut a woman, weary-looking with sad, frightened eyes, sat beside a boy who was lying on a grass mat on the floor. His feverish head was cushioned on a roll of filthy rags; his swollen forehead a sticky mess of dark, pussy blood. He had just been initiated, and the cuts had become infected. I imagined awful things, convinced on the spot that this was the result of heathenism, part of Satan's doings—part of the battle which must be won for Jesus Christ. This was the spiritual darkness the Bible speaks of, the manifestation of a bound people.

The boy recovered, but in the months and years which followed, my attitude did not improve; rather, it worsened, not from a deeper sense of pity for the deceived initiates, but from a personal, growing exasperation. I could never acquiesce to little schoolboys, sometimes no more than twelve years old, who with their marked foreheads would stiffen in defiance at some request of mine, saying, "I am a man" and refuse to do what I had asked. I was frustrated to irritation when adults insisted that a man would die if he milked a cow. The fear accompanying their insistence was proof to me of spiritual imprisonment, and if they could only be released, I thought, then they would be free. But I failed to see that in this rite there was order, not chaos. Instead, I argued with the people, and especially with the young men who came back from the secondary schools, dressed in their uniforms and looking very sophisticated and progressive, but I could get none of them to agree with me. "It is our custom, Nyarial," they would say. And Kuac also agreed with them, which was a blow to me, for I thought surely he would recognize the evil in it and condemn it to his people.

But after many years of exasperation, the first thing happened to help me understand. I was walking home from the village one afternoon with the mission nurse, when I met a girl who was crying. It was unusual for a girl to walk about crying.

"What is it?" I said.

She could hardly speak at first and tears were streaming down her cheeks.

"It is my brother, . . . he was bitten by a snake."

She sobbed.

I waited.

"When?"

"This morning. He was at the river."

Again she sobbed.

She turned her head and blew her nose on the ground. She stopped sobbing and relaxed a little.

"Which snake was it?"

"The red cobra," she said. "My brother went to the river to bathe. And the snake bit him. And when he was being taken to the 'house of magic,' which was the clinic, he died. We have just buried him."

Then she began to cry and sob again.

Crying was often staged. People cried ceremonially, or because they were afraid. But this girl was crying honestly, as if her heart would break. I groped in my mind for something relevant to say. I spoke to her of God, then stopped—I was off the track, I wasn't appreciating what had happened. But when she spoke again, then I understood.

"Had you seen him," she cried, "you would have known that he was truly a man. He was to be marked next year."

I knew now why she cried. It was because he did not get to become a *man*. He had died a boy. She had been robbed of an irreplaceable pride: her brother's manhood. His name had died with him because he was not a man, and herein he was lost—to her, to the family, and to the tribe. If the cobra had turned its head, and the year passed, and the initiation rite had been enacted, the boy would have become a man, and death, had it come, would not have annihilated him. As it was, he had been cut off. No child could be born to him; no one could bear his name.

Now, as I watched what was happening to Ruey, I tried to look past the blood and gore, past the heathenism, past all my preconceived notions to discover the significance of what was taking place. In five minutes a little boy was becoming a man. By becoming a man he would throw away his reed spear for a real one. He would follow the men when the cry went up to fight. He could be "murdered," a verb which was not applicable to anyone else, the significance being that only the life of a murdered man could and would be atoned for by the life of his enemy. The man's family would see to this. By becoming a man he would cease to mimic his older brothers, he would join them in the dance, albeit in a group of his own, with its own name, its own members, its own sequence in tribal history. He would leave, forever, the female domain where, until now, he had lived. He would not sleep in his mother's hut again. He would not milk cows. An imaginary line separated men from all things feminine, and over this line, if a man dared to step, awaited the penalty of death—not by man's hand but God's. Death was a disguised friend, for in that they feared it greatly, both sexes agreed to guard against any transgressing of that line. Hence, a boy was destined to become a man from the soul outward—every boy, be he crippled, deformed, dumb, blind. It was the pinnacle of human experience, shared vicariously by the women, and in this destiny the entire tribe sank its roots and profited. My culture had nothing to compare with it.

The initiation provided a strong foundation for the stability and continuum of the tribe. Thus a man's birthday was forgotten, but his initiation established him forever as a man.

But Ruey was not under the spell of all this just now, for a tear rolled from the corner of his eye, across his cheek, and dropped into the ashes. His mother watched the knife pierce to the skull, then lifted her head and looked away. The tear came and was gone. It brought forth no comment then, but I wondered if in some future fight, mention might not be made of it.

Man Gaac's reaction was a moment of truth for me melting the cold indifference which outwardly prevailed, and I felt akin to her again. As each line was carved, slashing the tender skin, bringing more blood, I tried to imagine how she must feel as a mother who had successfully reared her third son to manhood.

There was glory and fulfillment in what she had accomplished. Life was meaningful because of it. She was knowing a greater measure of womanhood than I or untold thousands of civilized single women would ever realize. She had something money, education, civilization could not buy. Nor was it Christianity that had given it to her. But it was God. God in heathenism. Try, if you can, to fathom Him, to draw His picture with clear, solid lines, to pin Him down. Just when you think you have God in focus, He moves, and the picture blurs.

I watched as the cutter turned from Ruey to the last boy. The scene was the same. There was no talking and no one but the cutter moved. The sun was becoming hot now, and the cattle were getting to their feet. When the cutter finished, he put down his cutting edge and got up. Three men knelt behind the initiates, shooing away the flies. A skinny, mouse-colored dog came sniffing toward us. One of the fly-shooing men flung out his hand and scared it away.

The cutter, who had gone to the barn and put on his cloth, now came back with a piece of shiny cornstalk husk in his hand. Kneeling down again beside the first boy he began gently scraping the ridges of coagulated blood standing thick on his forehead, dropping the blood into the ashes. He went from the one to the other and, as the blood smeared, the cuts gaped, leaving firey-looking foreheads gleaming in the sun. After the cutter finished, the boys were covered with three muslin cloths from head to toe, just as they lay, not yet moving a muscle.

The men waited for a time until they were sure the bleeding had subsided; then at the command from the cutter, the cloths were removed, and the first boy lifted himself off the ground with his hands, keeping his back parallel to the ground. With his head hanging down behind him, he pushed himself with his hands and feet, wheelbarrow fashion, toward the barn. The boy could not see where he was going and the cutter told him how to go: "Come to this side a little . . . go over to the right side a little . . . like that. Hold your head down!" The boy was not supposed to be supported

by any other person. With quite a bit of effort on his part, the boy
made it through the oval doorway into the darkness.

Ruey was next. He lifted himself in the same manner and
moved forward, haltingly. Man Gaac was behind him, bending
down as if in readiness to help if he collapsed. The cutter, in bel-
ligerent disagreement, told her to leave him alone. But Man Gaac
was not to be deterred. At the barn doorway she put her hands to
her son's shoulders, easing him across the threshold, she herself not
intending to enter, forbidden as she was to do so.

When the last boy disappeared into the barn, the ceremony was
over. No woman would be permitted to go into the barn until the
period of confinement of two weeks was over. On that day the three
initiates would come out, wearing leather "dunce" caps as protection to the fresh scars from the evil eye, and bracelets, beads, and
other fineries. Their bodies would be "full," as the people said. They
would walk together through the villages, carrying their spears and
clubs to be seen and accepted by the people as men.

Any man who was to take his place in the tribe must begin in
this way. If he did not first "become" a man, he could not become
anything else, for he would be only a boy. I thought of the man in
the pulpit—Kuac: pastor, teacher, translator. Without his marks, he
could have become none of these to his people. What I had once so
easily defined and rejected as a heathen practice had now formed
in my mind as a legitimate, meaningful act.

The telltale piles of dung ash, now blackened with the globs of
wet blood, were all that remained to show that a marking rite had
just occurred. Even these would disappear, disposed of in a manner fitting to the people's beliefs, lest leaving them carelessly about
might put the boys' lives in danger. Blood, shed in this way, was
very vulnerable.

To go home I had to walk back toward the river. Man Gaac had
to walk in the opposite direction, so we parted—not with words,
but with the realization that we had been together, that now it was
over and we must go. I had to pass by the cattle on my way home,

and in doing so I came upon another drama. Two men, wearing only beads and ivory bracelets, were standing by a young, black bull which they had hobbled and thrown to the ground. One man was holding its horns while the other, on his knees, castrated it with a knife of as crude design as the one used on the boys. Surely, I thought, this bull will begin to struggle and try to get away; but I was wrong. It behaved, instead, in a manner similar to that of the boys themselves. I watched, fascinated, interested to see that the atmosphere here was a casual one; the men were relaxed and talking with each other. Apparently, this was not as solemn a situation as the marking of the boys. Their one concern for me was that I not get too close, lest I get hurt should the bull decide to fight. I stepped to one side, not thinking especially of the danger involved, but of how fortunate I was to be seeing this, too. I remembered, later, having read about it. The book had said that sometimes a bull is castrated at the time of a boy's initiation, but for the moment I had forgotten this. It was only as I stood watching and concentrating on what was happening that the significance of the two acts came to me: This young bull was submitting to the act which would rob it of its manhood and ready it for possession by one of the initiates to whom it would be given, would share its name and, spiritually speaking, its life.

Lying in their huts, on a night of the full moon, the old people would rejoice to hear the song of the young man, whom they would picture dancing behind his black ox, parading on the plain, bedecked in the finery of youth, his neck bulging with multiple strands of giraffe-hair necklaces, colored beads at his waist, his left arm encased from wrist to elbow in a series of metal bracelets, an ivory bracelet on his other arm, his hair aflame, its tiny wiry ringlets bleached and straightened, now standing straight out like the head of a feathery dandelion. They might not hear his song, but they would know that he was singing of himself and of his life, of the girl he wanted, and of his ox. There with his ox, whose horns he had polished until the tips were shiny and smooth, he was singing to them of his manhood, which they projected in their minds to be his immortality. So they would go to sleep to the sweet tinkling of the ox's bell, which from its place below the animal's neck, swayed gently back and forth to the rhythm of the ox's slow, steady plod across the plain, knowing that this son of the tribe could never be lost to them.

2

INTO THE WHITE MAN'S WORLD

The school complex was located in the middle of the mission compound. The cook house and grain storehouse, where bats lived by the hundreds, were in line with the three dormitories. One of these was a thatched brick rectangular building; the rest were made of mud and sticks. This line of buildings formed one side of the large playing field which extended to the river. Joining that line of buildings at the back of the field were the three brick classrooms with wooden desks, each large enough for two boys to sit at, and the teachers' houses paralleling the river. Opposite the dormitories, across the playing field, was a small, oval brick building with a mud-wall partition in the middle dividing the building into two classrooms.

The missionaries lived on either side of the school unit. There were two residences on each side of the compound, with the clinic, church, and school between. There was also a brick storehouse behind one of the residences, an orchard, three windmill towers, two water storage tanks in the towers, and shade trees by all the buildings. Originally, the residences were all made of red brick, but one was later replaced by a concrete house with aluminum roofing. The clinic and church were brick too.

(In recent years, the government absorbed the boys' education and built a school of its own a mile and a half beyond the mission, upstream, past the government quarters. The old boys' school then became a government boarding school for girls.)

In the mission school in the 1940s there was a boy named Kuac. He was born in this land that lay flat on its back, was rolled out like a pie crust and crisscrossed with a network of footpaths, linking village with village, the imprint of a people who walk in order to communicate, and who must communicate in order to live. Over those paths go the messengers of tidings, good and evil: A child is born. A wife has died. The grain has been planted. A marriage dance has taken place. An ox has been killed in sacrifice. A cow is lost. A divorce has occurred. These paths wind through the grain fields, past village sites and head off across the open plains to villages beyond. They cut across swamps, under the still, brown water like a subway circuit, a trail of thick, slippery, bottomless mud. They meander under thorn trees, through scrub forests, and out across the miles of burned-off plain—dark lines over the land, twisting and turning around hummocks and ant hills and nothing at all. Countless crooked miles of footsteps, the mark of tough, human feet.

None of them is permanent. They change at the whim of the people. They follow no landmarks, for there are none to follow. Nothing bars them entrance, or denies them the right of way, and all men share them equally.

The mission and the village where Kuac was born were connected by a footpath like two beads on a string. From his village, Kuac could look out across the swamp and see the mission on the wide bend of the river with the windmill towers sticking up above the lone block of trees. But from the mission, the village was scarcely visible. Its round thatched huts and barns of mud and sticks stood like mushrooms in a thin line along the river's edge, bared to the blaze of the sun, as though they had sprouted and grown up there. Where the village began there was a tree, gray-barked with thick, gnarled branches and tough, dusty leaves with beads and a few metal bracelets hanging among them, offerings to God. The village was sprawled along the bank of a meandering tributary of the Sobat River, which flowed out of Ethiopia and into the White Nile, two hundred miles to the northwest at Malakal, the government headquarters of the Upper Nile Province of the Sudan.

It was a silent river, looping its way through the grass, brushing against the long-stemmed reeds, making them sway gently as it passed, flowing over sand and clay. To the Nuer people it was the water they drank, the place they bathed, their provider of fish, and it hid one of their greatest enemies, the crocodile. If the river did not rise properly, the people prayed. If it flooded, they prayed. If it had no fish, they gave it an ox.

Because of the river there were the migrating birds that came to feed on frogs and fish and insects. Great water birds, like the giant heron that flew alone, its long, auburn-feathered neck retracted in the shape of a Z, its gray legs stretched out behind like the legs of a diver. It pulled itself through the air with the deep, graceful movements of its mammoth, silver-gray wings always on the lookout, turning its head from side to side and sounding its deep, agitated squawk in the manner of a disgruntled, overbearing lord.

The white heron also came. It was smaller and moved more quickly, as though the far side of the world were its destination and it were a lady going there.

One afternoon, just as the sun was setting and when, in the west a large cloud layer had left only a slit for the sun to peep through, I chanced to glance up at the precise moment of one of these maiden's flights across the sky. I saw a white heron in gorgeous pink, a gift from the sun, whose rays of pink and rose had transformed the white bird into a flaming flamingo flying against a background of rosy gray cloud.

The black-and-white terns came to the river in squadrons and skimmed its glassy surface with swept-back wings, scoring the water with their bills as they drank on the wing, never slowing down, wings beating in perfect harmony, first turning to the left, then to the right, then soaring into the air again to circle and return in a swooping dive to make a zigzag flight back upstream.

The tall, eccentric Maribou storks, hunched over and decrepit-looking, stood sulkily on the riverbank on skinny, gray legs. But when they took to the air, they would climb up and up until they were almost out of sight, and there on cushions of air they would ride, on outstretched wings, round and round in effortless flight, a company of paper-thin witches, black specks in the sky.

The boy Kuac, who came to the mission school, knew the birds and river, but not as I did. He understood them in one way; I understood them in another. He became the key to unlock for me his people's view of God and the world.

Kuac resembled his mother, a short, fine-featured woman whose two front teeth were slightly separated. What little I ever saw of her confirmed Kuac's appraisal of her that she was a quiet-spoken woman who never fussed or became angry even if, as had occurred, another woman had taken her water pot and broken it.

His father, Kuac said, was a kind man as he remembered him, whom the people respected for his fairness in dealing with quarrels. He had had two wives and five children—three sons and two daughters. Kuac was the second eldest son and fourth child. There had been a lot of preaching and evangelizing done in the village, but Nyot, Kuac's father, was not interested. He insisted that he had only one God, *Kuoth nhial,* the God of the sky, and that was all he needed. It was Nyot who gave Kuac his name, which means "leopard," and by doing this he honored a friend who had brought him a gift of a leopard skin on the day Kuac was born.

Nyot died before Kuac was very old. It was his mother who permitted him to go to the mission-sponsored village school in his own village. There he learned to read from crayoned flash cards and to write with his finger in the dust, then later with chalk on a mission-made blackboard propped against the thatch.

When he had learned sufficiently well, his mother allowed him to go to the mission boarding school. There he met the white man whom everyone called "chief," and was given a cloth, called a *kar,* for his own—a rectangular piece of white muslin brought around the shoulders like a toga, and tied.

"Take off your fighting bracelet," the white man said, meaning the many-pronged metal bracelet boys wore, "and put on this cloth. You are in class one. Here is your mosquito net. Here is your blanket. Here is your soap. You will live in the big house with the other boys." Like everybody else, Kuac was attracted to the mission school by the material benefits it afforded. There were no fees to cover the cost of all they were given: daily food, a cloth to wear and to keep, soap, medicine, and the privilege of sleeping with blankets under mosquito nets. Kuac stayed four years and did well. But although he was quick to learn the value of the things he was given, which attracted him to the missionaries, what he did not learn was the cost of soap and mosquito nets and blankets, and how having them increased one's appetite for other things.

Instinctively, the missionary wanted the boys to have what he had, but he wanted them to get it honestly, with their own hands. The country's poverty appalled him and typically of the white man, when he came to live in the country, he immediately began to conquer it. So he felt the African would follow suit, with a little encouragement. I was certainly all for this in my early days in Africa, but one day Kuac happened to mention that first white man he had known. He said, "He was a good man," and getting up from his chair, with his shoulders hunched forward slightly, he demonstrated how the tall, heavyset Dane would walk down the path with his large basket of fruit, the schoolboys trailing him.

"Boys," Kuac said, husking his voice to resemble the missionary's, "run, chase those goats out of the garden and I will give you these guavas in my basket."

"And we would listen, frightened at his strong voice, then we would run away to chase the goats and return quickly to pick up the guavas he had spilled out on the ground, and eat them."

The boys liked the smooth, yellow-skinned fruit with the sweet, pink insides. There was nothing like it in the village, nothing sweet. And if guavas were good, they thought oranges were better. But all fruit trees had to be irrigated, and in the dry season, when the sun baked the earth bone-dry, the villagers moved to the swamps with their cattle and no one was left in the village.

"He was a good man," Kuac repeated. "'Boys,' he would say, 'you like guavas, don't you?'

"'*Uh*,' we would say.

"'That is good. Now listen to my word. This earth, it is your earth, is it not?'

"'*Uh*,' we would say.

"'And the guava trees are growing in this earth, is it not so?'

"'*Uh*.'

"'So what does this mean? You see it means that each of you can have his own guava tree, is it not so?'

"We would all say, '*Uh*,' then he would walk away."

"And did anybody have a tree?" I asked.

"No," Kuac answered, "it is impossible."

At first I thought that type of attitude simply reflected a lazy, disinterested kind of people. But as the years passed I learned that Kuac was right, that it was impossible to keep trees alive unless you had a harem of women to carry water, or the wherewithal to finance the purchase, running, and upkeep of machinery.

At the mission Kuac was taught about God and Jesus Christ. He learned that there was no merit in animal sacrifice, that Jesus was the true sacrifice and the one, true God. He learned that one day in seven was called *cang Kuoth*—day of God—and that on that day there was no formal work done at the mission; that is, the workmen did not report for duty although the houseboys did, and in the middle of the morning when the work bell did ring, it was time to go to the *duel Kuoth*—house of God. Kuac went to church because all the schoolboys were lined up and expected to go and sit together in their mission-issued cloths. This made him part of the group, a class in itself, including the clinic dressers, the garden workers, houseboys, and to some degree the in-patients who made up the morning congregation.

The "talk of God" which the white man taught went along with reading, writing, and arithmetic—these things found on the paper—the paper by which the white man lived and got his wealth. To attain to a status like the white man's, or at least to have what he had—money, clothes, greatness, power, and so forth—it was logical that a boy should not only accept the reading, writing, and arithmetic, but the Bible talk too, since who was to know just where the secret of the white man's success lay? Therefore, since the sign of a Christian was baptism, hundreds of schoolboys had been baptized through the years. This was not necessarily a decisive spiritual act, because in the Nuer mind one's relationship to God was inconsequential until he reached adulthood. It was then, as a responsible member of family and clan, one's beliefs were laid on the line.

This is not to say that some of the decisions were not sincere. It is to say that, in adulthood, baptized adolescents were often overpowered by the pressure of death and the group—then Christianity and baptism were forgotten.

Baptism was not a discernible Christian rite either. Putting water on the head and saying God's name was similar to the hocus-pocus performed by prophets and sorceresses.

In spite of these things, there were those boys whose confession seemed genuine. Kuac was one of them. He wrote of his experience later, explaining his state of mind at the time:

"When I came to the school my years were fourteen. I knew writing and reading. We read the Bible books. When my years were eighteen, the missionary called me before him and said that my head should be washed in the name of God.

"I said to him, 'Oh chief, my head cannot be washed now while my relative is away.' But that was not really what I meant. The big thing to me was I was afraid because something was still the matter with me, I had not turned myself around well. But he insisted that I should not wait for my relative. He said, 'Go, think about it for these days.'

"During those days I was persuaded by the other boys that my head should be washed. I said, 'Yes, it will be so.'

"When the day of washing arrived my head was washed with the rest. At the time I became a *Krithien mi koc koc* [a soft Christian]. I loved cursing and other kinds of playing around, which did not line up with the way of a Christian. [As far as I could ever tell, Christian behavior patterns were outlined by the missionaries and were not born out of the Africans' own experience with God.]

"I grew in a bad way, but the love of God was not finished in me.

"When the time of my young manhood arrived I desired girls very much. Then I sinned a sin which was about a girl. I slept with a girl who had previously slept with a relative of ours. In our country this is not good. When I realized what I had done, in the morning fear came over me so as to kill me. The people were surprised. Fear put my head in confusion like a person who wakes up crazy. Then I sinned again. I left God. I went after the works of evil. I went to a prophet so that my trouble would be over, so that he would kill a sheep by splitting it in two, which is the work of a prophet for this kind of mistake.

"When I returned from the sacrifice I knew I had sinned before God, but I did not know how my sin could go away. After a few days I got a disease called *relapthing piber* [relapsing fever]. During that sickness I began to think that if I should die, where would I go? I knew surely that no person could go to God if he did not go by the path of Jesus. God would not agree to a person's going to His country without permission. I then attached myself to the Lord [that word he wrote in English; the rest I have translated from Nuer] as my God, at that time and continuing onward. God could surely worry about all the people He created on the earth that each person's powers would not be directed to what He wants. God put me in His work because He knew that on that path my heart would be happy."

Following his schooling at the mission, Kuac became a teacher there. He continued to plant and hoe his field, to go fishing and attend the marriage dances for his friends. He was popular among them because of his friendly nature and his ability to sing. But at the same time he came faithfully to the church and became increasingly interested in things spiritual. He had no doubts that Jesus was God, that the Bible was the Word of God. Of course, he had no doubts about airplanes or radios, either. He desired to learn English and succeeded, in that eventually it became a second language to him.

3

THY BROTHER'S BLOOD

The year after Kuac had finished his elementary schooling at the mission, I looked down from the slow-moving river boat one day at the tall, naked black people looking up at me. They were standing under the glaring sun in a clearing where there were stacks of neatly piled firewood, a small wizened tree, and an Arab merchant's square, mud hut. To either side of the clearing the green river reeds covered the land as far as you could see in a wide band up and downstream, and behind the band of reeds was the thorn forest, dwarfed by the vastness of the empty plain.

There was a shrill, deafening blast of the whistle and the gaping people stepped back; the children looked at each other and giggled. Shouts went back and forth from boat to shore.

The boat nudged the bank, and chunks of black earth plunked into the water. A sailor jumped off with a cable in his hands and tugged at it, dragging it up the bank, his back bending, and wound it round the little tree. The paddlewheels churned, the water foamed, the bell in the engine room clanged, and then the motor stopped and the quiet wheels dripped water. There had been a cool breeze on board as long as we were moving; now it was gone. The voices of the people and the bleating of the sheep filled the hot, heavy air. Down on the barge the wooden-cleated gangplank was pushed over the side onto the bank, and an Arab went ashore wearing an orange skullcap and a white *jelabeeya*, like a man's nightshirt, the hem of which he had picked up and now held between his teeth. On the shore another Arab met him. They embraced, hanging their chins over each other's shoulders, and said their lengthy greetings into the air.

The clearing was full of people milling about who had just come off the boat. Men began to bathe in the river. Soapsuds floated downstream. Below me, on the barge, a woman sat hunched over a blackened pot on a hissing three-legged pressure stove. I could watch her by leaning over the railing. Behind her a man butchered a chicken, plucked it, and pushed its scalded feathers overboard with his bare feet. A boy let down an empty pail into the river, drawing it up again full of brown water.

Tall Africans, with gunny sacks on their shoulders, began loading their naked backs with firewood and came on board. We were taking on wood to fire the engine for the rest of the journey. The air rumbled as their loads fell onto the steel-plated deck. Burdening and unburdening themselves, they kept coming and going to and from the boat all afternoon, unperturbed, without haste, laughing and nagging and shouting at one another intermittently in the most relaxed manner.

The two Arabs were now by the square hut, sitting in deck chairs with low-slung canvas, in the frail shade of the wizened tree, talking. A thin shadow fell across their laps and faces, leaving their skirted legs and bare feet in the bright sunlight. As they talked a young girl came out from the house, wearing an unevenly hemmed orange dress, designed like a child's slip, plain, with built-up shoulders. The miserable dress hung on her straight, curveless body like a sack. She carried a small, wooden table and put it down in front of the men. Then she returned to the house and came out again with a brightly embroidered cloth, which she fixed on the table so that one corner dipped much closer to the ground than the others.

She disappeared, to come again with a large tray that she put on the table for the men, an enamel bowl of stew ringed with several pieces of *kisera,* the flappy Arab sour bread which is folded into triangles and has the appearance of sand-colored napkins.

The sun was halfway from zenith to the horizon when the whistle blew again, summoning the passengers back on board. The

Arabs had finished their meal and tea; the stacks of wood were gone. A donkey lifted his head and brayed at the far side of the hut, wheezing and gasping as donkeys do, and finished in a state of exhaustion. The whistle blew a second time. The passengers were coming back on board, the clearing was emptying, the two Arabs were embracing and saying their last farewells. Then the engine began to throb, the sailors brought in the cable, and the paddle-wheel swished loudly in the water. Slowly, we moved backward into the stream.

From midstream, the clearing looked remote again. The wood-carriers were leaving the scene—tall, lean men, a few of them distinguished by a strange assortment of scant, ill-fitting clothing. On the bank the Arab merchant stood watching with his little boy. It was the end of the show for them. As we moved upstream, the door of the square hut came into view, and there a thick-set Arab woman stood watching us, too. Two small children, in dirty undershirts, clutched at her knees. She stooped and lifted one into her arms, then as the distance between us lengthened and our boat approached a bend, she turned and went into the house.

It was December 1949. In January 1956, the Sudan was to get its independence from Britain. I was twenty-four and just out of college. I was on my way to Nasir as a missionary and these were the first Africans I had ever seen, sweat gleaming on their bodies, voices ringing out, faces soft and with changing expressions. They were not like the pictures of them I had seen, standing in rows, statuesque, all looking alike either as "schoolboys" or as "pagans." And as naturally as when I was in college making friends, I wanted to know these people, too. I was full of excitement that day, nerved with the hope of helping these people, confident that life could and would be better for them. It never crossed my mind then that my definition of their need was meaningless to them, that for all practical purposes I would have to invent a need in order to validate the message I had come to give. Nor was I prepared to give them the kind of help they wanted; for example, to make barren women fruitful, or to cause a plentiful harvest.

This was the first day of a three-day river journey of nearly two hundred miles to Nasir from the provincial capital at Malakal. A missionary couple, their three children, and I were the only first-class passengers on board the barge of the *Beatrice,* a small, wood-burning sternwheeler. We had the top of the living barge to ourselves. We did our own catering, boiling the river water, drinking tea, and eating canned food and fruit. We read and wrote letters in the screened-in front deck, and stood by the railing for hours on end watching the river and scanning the plain, looking for crocodiles and hippopotami and wild animals, but we saw none.

The river was at its annual peak, overflowing its banks and inundating the land. Unhindered, it turned the plain into an unnavigable network of lakes and swamps. In another month, as I was to see, the river would begin to recede, draining the land, and the sun would then bake it hard, drying it up until it shriveled and cracked, and the cracks would grow and gape open and go deep into the ground. Then the tall grass, once green and tender, would stand brittle and brown, and the fires would come and burn off great sections of the grass, blackening the earth, charring the plain, and clouding the sky with black, ashy filament carried on the wind. In the rush of the liquid flames, the scarlet bee-eaters and the fork-tailed kites would dart in and out of the heat, ahead of the fire, snatching at insects, hurling themselves at the wind. Purged, the earth would then lie naked to the sun until the months passed and the rains came back, and the swollen rivers overflowed on the plain—and the land would live again.

Nasir was on a wide bend of the river. Behind it was the local village of Kuanylualthoaan. Upstream from the mission and continuing as though one with it were the merchant quarters and the government offices. Across the river was the empty plain, green in the rainy season, and faded brown in the dry season, and on the far horizon a small village whose flickering firelights were sometimes visible on still, black nights.

From the river, the mission buildings were half hidden in the trees. As we came toward it, children gathered in places along the bank, and as we came parallel with them, they ran with us to the dock. There was a blast on the whistle, the engines were throttled back, and we came in slowly, hitting the bank. The dock area was full of people, standing and squatting, staring at the boat, and men of officialdom in khaki uniforms, off by themselves, looking very knowing and ready to give commands. As soon as the boat was secured, the engines were silenced and the gangplank put down; then people began going ashore. First the Arab merchant, pompous and full of expectancy, then schoolboys, home for the holidays, in khaki shorts and shirts, carrying their possessions in wooden or metal padlocked boxes on their heads; Arab women, fat and cumbersome, swathed in muslin of ink-blue or black and semiveiled, with shiny black, plastic slipperlike shoes, and little children in tow and native servants following, loaded down with boxes and bedrolls stacked on their heads; nattily dressed policemen with rifles and smartly polished leather sandals, coming as replacements for men now going on leave; women in cotton prints and braided hair with babies on their hips and larger children in new, oversized outfits, followed by barefooted servant boys in white undershirts and khaki shorts bringing the chickens tied by their feet, the boxes, muslin sacks, and paraphernalia of African travel.

In the middle of the crowd, on the shore, stood a stout, white woman, her gray hair showing under her brown pith helmet, fixed in a roll at the back of her head, and wearing thick, metal-rimmed glasses, blue anklets and black, cuban-heeled shoes, and a blue print cotton dress. She was the elder missionary whose imminent retirement created the vacancy I had come to fill as an evangelist among the village people. She was presently joined by three other women from the mission, two of whom I knew, and at their coming I left the boat.

My friends hailed my arrival with much merriment and put a lei of oleander blossoms around my neck. The older woman soon excused herself, saying that she had a literacy class of adults to teach, inviting me to stop at her house to see her when I got to the mission. We said goodbye to her and she went away, acknowledging with short nods the greetings of the people.

We left the dock and went down the hard, clay road past the merchants, toward the mission, following the mission workmen who were carrying my baggage and food supplies I had brought with me from Malakal. The road was straight, built up in the middle to facilitate drainage, with wide ditches on either side. It was not a proper automobile road; it was used mainly for the people, since lorries were few and far between, and not seen at all in the rainy season.

Neem trees lined both sides of the road, shading the mud shops with their flat roofs of corrugated sheet metal and open corrugated metal doors. Each shop was a little grotto with a counter and a back wall, shelved, and displaying bolts of muslin, khaki and cotton prints, tea, matches, ballpoint pens, and an assortment of faded and dusty odds and ends. Hanging on the inside of the open doors were strings of colored beads of varying sizes and shapes, and metal bracelets in clusters. Outside, under the roof extensions, grain was piled on the ground for selling. Arab proprietors lounged in deck chairs in the shade while natives wandered aimlessly up and down gazing into the open shops.

At the end shop a woman stooped to lift an oblong basket of grain. Hoisting it to her knee, she repositioned her hands at each end, enabling her then to lift the basket up and duck under it so that the basket was finally sitting on top of her head. After that she walked away, steadying the basket with her right hand held high, her left arm free at her side. She stepped firmly with bare feet on the smooth, hot clay, her thin neck and back bearing the weight, feeling the sun. As she walked, her tapered, leather loincloth swayed gently against her straight, black legs to the motion of her lean hips. Dignified, self-possessed, unsophisticated, I respected her.

At the corner, where the road stopped, the woman turned and went toward the village. We continued straight ahead, crossing a ditch, through a hedge, onto the compound of the American Mission, belonging to the United Presbyterian Church of North America. The mission had a ninety-nine-year lease from the Sudan government for the property and had already been established there for fifty years.

It was at Nasir that I was to meet Kuac, and to work with him for the next thirteen years, until the Sudan government initiated a drastic program culminating in the expulsion of all missionaries from the south Sudan.

But on this hot December day I did not know Kuac, nor did I know what the future held. I was only aware that I was finally in Africa, prepared to spend my life here. I could not, like Cain, deny that these people were my brothers. I bore a heavy response, which if I shirked, would leave their blood on my hands.

4

HE WHO HATH EARS TO HEAR

At six thirty on each weekday morning, with the sun well above the earth and shining brightly, I opened the metal gate to the elder missionary's yard and walked up the path. Seeing me from the table where she worked by her large bedroom window, she would slide back her chair, and coming to the screen door of the veranda, meet me as I arrived.

"*Mal mi goaa?*" she would say, greeting me—Is it good peace?

And I would dutifully answer, "*Uh, e mal mi goaa*"—Yes, it is good peace.

Then I would eat my breakfast at her table, she herself sitting by me, having eaten alone an hour earlier. As I ate she talked, telling me stories about herself, the mission, and her colleagues, past and present. She had been a nurse but was devoting all of her time to village evangelism. Now that I had come she assumed the responsibility for my initiation into missionary life, and for my language study. Unsure that I would make sufficient progress out of her sight, she had arranged for me to begin my language work on her veranda each morning. However, in all of the time I spent there with her we never discussed the language together.

My lesson was at seven. The "teacher" whom she had engaged was a baptized schoolboy who also served as one of the missionary's paid village evangelists. His name was Riek. It meant "trouble." His contribution to my beginning days at language learning was twofold: he was patient, and he knew enough English to be able to translate simple words such as *cow*, *house*, *river*, and so forth. In that a grammar of the language was not available, and there were no books other than a few translations of parts of the Bible and some elementary schoolbooks, and no Nuer qualified to teach a foreigner the language, daily progress was slow.

Each day at eight, the lesson over, the older woman would come out to the veranda to brief Riek on the village trip for the day, give him his cloth bag she had made to hold the notebook she had sewn together for the names of the villagers who wanted to be "written," and a pencil to check the attendance. Being written meant having one's name entered and checked each week for faithful attendance. Then, if after a certain period of time of faithful attendance, the individual could satisfy the examining board of missionary and church elders by answering correctly to questions relating to Jesus Christ and salvation, he would be baptized. Riek's messages and the prayer he always prayed were taught to him by the missionary who hoped that in this way no falsehoods could creep in to distort the true Bible story.

I went with Riek to the village for what was called my practical language experience. We followed a footpath, he going ahead. The ground was dry and bare, baked by the sun, swept by the wind. It was December, the beginning of the season the Nuer called *jiom,* or wind. A most frustrating time of year when the north wind blows all day, drying the pools, burning the grass, driving the clouds out of the sky. The only creature I could see that seemed to enjoy it was the kite, which met the wind with all its power, riding into it, circling around it, diving through it, quivering above it, dashed by it, always careless, playful, asking for more, never tiring, screeching with the thrill of it, challenged by the strength of it. I would watch the kite for hours, zooming and climbing with it, swooping and colliding with it, wishing that he were I and that I were he.

As I walked, the wind whipped at my skirt and blew back the muslin cloth Riek wore, baring his body. It blew in our faces and at our backs, frolicking endlessly. There was nothing in its way; it was everywhere, disarranging, scattering, raising the dust.

Each hut and yard had a cornstalk fence around it. It was a relief to go inside and get away from the wind. We always sat down in the sun, against the fence, and waited until the people came and sat with us. "We have come to pray," Riek would say. (The word for "pray" was the Nuer kind of praying, the sacrifice. There was no other kind of prayer, so there was no other word for it.) Eventually, a few people would amble over to where we were. It was not compulsory; everyone did not have to come and sometimes there were people who refused. I wondered why. Afraid, perhaps.

Riek would take out his notebook and pencil and read off the names registered in this particular place. No one else there had a paper. No one else had a pencil. No one else could read and write.

After checking the names, Riek would say, "*E jen,*" which indicated a change of subject. Then he would say, "Let us pray. Let us bend our heads down." He would bow his head, and the people would watch him and bow their heads accordingly. It was a foreign act to them. Then Riek would pray, reproducing the foreign intonation pattern of the missionary's flawlessly.

The prayer said in part, "God, our Father, You are truly God. There is no other God. You are greater than everything. You are stronger than other gods. We have all sinned. Wash our hearts." After the prayer he would sing a song and some of the people would usually join in. The song said, "Come, Jesus, come. I am blind. You will open my eyes. I want you. I am blind. Take my hand. Show me your house. I want you. I want you."

After the song was over he told the Bible story, and after that he said the Lord's Prayer, which the people whose names were written were supposed to learn and say with him.

Then we would leave and go to the next place on the route. If there was a newborn baby at any place, Riek would mark that in his book and tell the missionary, who would visit the mother and give the baby a flannel cloth.

At the weekly mission prayer meeting, the elderly missionary would give the figure of how many villagers had heard the Gospel that week, which was included in a report she sent home to the mission board at the end of the year.

I was appalled by this system. I did not think the Gospel should be peddled. I expected God to appoint men to the job. I was incredulous that after fifty years of missionary work among these people, there was no striking hunger on the villager's part to hear the Gospel. I wondered where the people were who reportedly were crying out for the Word of God. Something must be wrong, I thought. Why is God not working? I was determined more than ever to learn the language, to know the people and tell them myself all I knew of Jesus Christ. I wanted them to "taste and see that the Lord is good."

Riek's help was exhausted in a few months. I passed my first language exam given by the elder missionary and fell heir, for a time, to the overseeing of the boys' school, an assignment long since predicted with the educationist's furlough due and no one to take her place. The combination of events put me on a different footing with my superior, and I became free to study language and eat breakfasts at home.

I studied at a homemade table at one end of the long veranda of our red brick bungalow overlooking the river. Between the veranda and the river was a wide yard, divided by a path going from the front door to a bougainvillea arbor at the river's edge. On either side of the path, shading the house, were two large poinciana trees, whose branches met overhead, making a canopy across the bare yard. The bright sunlight would come sifting down through the lacy leaves of the spreading trees, warming the veranda and making shadows on the clay. On the river, pieces of sudd frequently floated by, sometimes carrying a white heron, stiff-legged and alert, ready for instant flight.

Sitting at the table I would prop my feet against the cement ledge running along the veranda's edge framing the screen, and look at the language data I had accumulated. How was I to find the rhyme and reason to the words?

Nyal, meaning "girl," changes to *nyaal,* then to *nyieer,* then to *nyieet. Luak,* meaning "barn," changes to *luaak,* then to *lueek. Duel,* meaning "house," changes to *duëël,* then to *dueel,* then to *duël,* and finally to *duëli.* Were these noun changes classifiable? Given a noun, were its changes predictable? Or was this to remain an elusive language, conquered only by the memorization of each word change? I would hear the houseboys in conversation and interruptions at the back door, and despair of ever being able to separate the flow of soft, musical sounds into words and phrases.

I would sit with schoolchildren under the trees, practicing sounds, looking in their mouths to see how they said things, trying to ask questions, trying to understand. But I made little progress until I came to know Kuac. I hired him as my teacher upon recommendation by several of the missionaries at the station.

He was a teacher in the boarding school in those days, and he would come to the house wearing a pair of locally made shorts dyed navy blue, and a navy blue cloth tied at his shoulder which hung down to his knees like a toga. He had no shoes, no shirt, and his smooth, black chest showed a heavy scarred design made by picking up the skin with a thorn and nicking it with a sharp piece of metal or razor blade.

He was a small man for a Nuer, a little under six feet tall, about my height, with fine features and an almost exaggerated military posture. There was no fat on him. He was quick to laugh, a quiet, happy laugh, and to show his straight, white teeth which he walked about brushing with a piece of green branch chewed into a brush at one end, the size of a pencil.

He always wore a string of flat, light-blue beads at his waist; and around his forehead, sometimes garnished with a sprig of red bougainvillea, a string of smaller, black-and-white beads. He wore small circlets of giraffe-tail hair in his ears, and another larger circlet around his neck. There was always an ivory band around his left upper arm, lined with pitch so that it did not slide up and down, and a metal bracelet on his wrist.

He would never come into our house without a covering, even though a man in the village, before entering a hut, throws off his cloth and goes in without it. Every Nuer who had been connected with the mission had this westernized sense of modesty, created, I presume, by their observation of us and by the fact that all employees, except garden workers, were given clothes to wear. As a Nuer, Kuac was as innocent of the social disgrace of nakedness as was our houseboy who served the food at the table one night in his beads and a transparent, plastic apron.

Clothes were impractical, indeed for the most part unobtainable. They were not required for warmth, neither were pockets a necessity, since tobacco could be stuck behind the ear, and a coin, if needed, could be fitted in the ear, or carried in one's mouth. And what else was there to put in pockets? Only married women had a moral responsibility to be covered. But the wearing of beads was significant for everyone. A person's body was referred to as being "empty" or "full," depending upon whether you were wearing beads or not. One strand of beads around the waist was enough to meet this requirement. Whether you had clothes on or not was immaterial. It was the beads that counted. A baby, at birth, was not given a cloth, but beads were put around its ankles instead. The word *naked* did not occur in the Nuer vocabulary.

Kuac did not know much English, but what he knew he used, and together we corrected each other's speech. The learning process became more like a game or a continual discovery instead of painful necessity. Kuac had a natural linguistic ability, an aggressive spirit, uncurbed curiosity, and limitless patience. He had a perfect ear for the sounds of languages. He could isolate one sound and tell me how it should be said. This is impressive in a language of fourteen vowels, with combinations of diphthongs and triphthongs which could sustain four possible modifications, including three levels of tone, a variation of three different lengths, and the possibility of either a tense or lax quality.

The majority of words in the language were monosyllabic and occurred in a consonant-vowel-consonant pattern. Hence a vowel which underwent any of these modifications caused the meaning of the word to change or a grammatical change of the word itself.

It was Kuac's genius to be able to differentiate between these factors, developing his skill to the point where he was able to explain to me exactly what composed the sound of a given word, or how similar-sounding words differed.

He taught me more about his language and his people than any other person. He understood them both. He was not ashamed of his people, and his unusual confidence in the white man allayed any suspicions or fears he might have had of us.

I knew Kuac for thirteen years. He was never crude nor impolite. He enjoyed being with white people and seemed always to be able to adapt to them, to their conversation, to their questions. He distinguished himself to me by his frank opinions, his appreciation for learning, and his unspoiled attitude toward Jesus Christ. He spoke of Jesus Christ as a living being.

Neat little Christian phrases like being born again, or being burdened, or being blessed were not sayable in Nuer; hence one could not hide behind a blur of clichés. So in talking with Kuac, you had to say what you meant. You had to work hard to express yourself, to get to the bottom of things, using words that weren't geared to spiritual ideas. Then you had to work hard to understand his point of view; you had to listen and listen, and many times you would say, But why? and the marvel of it was that he could often tell you so that you understood.

Talking together was like having a sieve through which we strained our thoughts, and as long as we were honest with each other we could admit to what we did not know and discard the false concepts. This built a bridge between us, spanning both our cultures, which never collapsed.

5

EGGS, SNAKES, AND TWINS

It was taboo to eat any kind of fowl or their eggs. In a land where geese flock in fields by the hundreds and ducks whistle overhead in numberless waves, where guinea fowl, francolin, and bustard walk freely over the plain, it was singularly tragic that the people went hungry every year. But in their attempt to explain the phenomenon of multiple birth, the Nuer had concluded that twins come from birds. Thus in respect for the creature, and in fear of the Creator, they would not eat them or their eggs.

I unwittingly frightened a woman nearly to death on the path one day by offering her two game birds when she begged a coin from me. She was so surprised at my offer and at the birds I held in my hand, which I had just shot and she had not seen, that she ran away.

"Where are you going? What is the matter?" I called after her.

"She is a twin," she called back, stopping long enough to answer me, and pointing with her tongue to a woman coming toward me from the opposite direction whom I had not noticed before. As she approached me I held out the birds to her, saying, "Here, take these." Whereupon she too gave a little cry and, stepping out of my way, ran after her companion.

Each facet of tradition had its host of qualifying and complicating taboos. My initial reaction to taboos was total exasperation. To me, what the people did was devil-inspired trumpery, and illogical to boot. It was frustrating to discover eventually that my kind of logic did not demolish these illusory notions. And it was painful and disappointing to be making friends with people for whom my ideas were nonsense. The more I came to know them, the more I realized the barrier of taboos between us. But my disappointment went deeper. It stemmed from the fact that God was not shining in the darkness as I had prayed and hoped for and expected.

The Scriptures explained the basic problem to my satisfaction. It says in the Psalms: "They know not, neither will they understand; they walk on in darkness. All the foundations of the earth are out of course." I expected God to correct this situation. Had not Jesus said just before He died, "It is finished"? Did not that mean, in part at least, that what He had accomplished freed men to know God? That he "had delivered them who through fear of death were all their lifetime subject to bondage"?

St. Paul likened us Gentiles to "dead fetuses." Dead fetuses cannot hear. How then can men understand the Gospel? God Himself said in the Old Testament, "And I will give them a heart to know me, that I am the Lord." . . . "I shall speak and the word that I shall speak shall come to pass." . . . "Is not my word like a fire, and like a hammer?" God had said this to Israel. He meant it for them. But did He not mean it for others as well? For, I believed, if God did not make men understand, I could not.

"Turn thou us unto Thee, O Lord, and we shall be turned," cried the prophets Ezekiel and Jeremiah, and I echoed their cry.

Twins were not despised; they were treated in a special way. They were protected with elaborate taboos. If baby twins died before cutting their first teeth, they were not buried; they were put in a tree or on a hut roof to be given back to the birds.

One Sunday afternoon, the mission nurse and I sat quietly in an outpatient hut of the clinic. An elderly man, his head shaven and a string of beads at his waist, and an old woman with a few corroborators sat in a circle holding a conference. In the background, on the floor, was a young woman covered with a cloth, who had been delivered of twins the day before. One of the twins had died. The old man held in his hand short slivers of dried grass. Laying them on the floor of the hut in two piles, he enumerated the gifts due to each child. This is a bracelet, he would say, putting a sliver down, this is for beads. These gifts, I supposed, were to have been forthcoming from relatives, and must be divided evenly for the living child's sake. They were "owed" no doubt to the children, special gifts given to twins. After everyone was satisfied that each gift had been remembered and accounted for by the straws, the man then paused, somewhat puzzled, and looked at the nurse, saying, "Where will the child be taken?"

Knowing their custom, she suggested either of two places, the only places in fact, close by, where there were any trees; either the orchard or the bamboo grove across the river.

"No, it will not be taken to the orchard." They all agreed that it was too public. "It will be taken across," they said, meaning across the river.

"Will it be good there?" an old woman ventured.

"*Uh*, it will be good," the old man said.

"How will we go?" they asked.

"We will take you," the nurse said, anticipating the experience.

A storm was brewing in the south as the four of us climbed into the aluminum boat. A strong wind was roughing the water, lifting the surface into tiny white caps. The sky had turned a purplish-gray. The old people were afraid. They each held on to the gunwhale with one hand and clutched their cloths around them with the other. "Where is the paddle?" the old woman asked instinctively.

"No. It has a machine," the old man answered her.

Crossing to the other side, we tied the boat and climbed the bank to the grove. The wind had quieted down. The man went ahead, surveying the tall bamboos. The old woman followed, carrying the child in a small, round gourd. Deciding on a particular clump of bamboo, the man threw off his cloth and climbed up the long, springy stems.

"It is so," he said when he had found a place, and reaching down took the gourd which the old woman, who had climbed part way into the clump, was handing up to him. With our heads tilted skyward as far as they would go, we watched him anchor the little gourd. An interlacing network of small, leafy branches made a canopy over it. And thousands of nesting weaverbirds kept up a dinning dirge. The man looked back over his head as he climbed down to the ground, satisfying himself that all was well. The old woman took the slivers of grass representing the gifts belonging to the dead child and pushed them carefully into the bottom of the clump. Straightening herself again, she looked up at the gourd. "You stay here," she said kindly, "and your brother will stay across the river. God will protect you."

Then we left and went back to the other side.

Whom did she mean? If you had asked her she might have said "*Kuoth.*" *Kuoth* meant God. As a verb it meant to blow as one does when blowing out a candle, or blowing up a fire, but it could not be used for the wind. She may have explained herself so far as to say *Kuoth caka,* the creating God, or *Kuoth nhial,* the God who is up there. This is all one being of whom the people knew very little. They thought He was good, but they seldom thought of Him.

If the old woman had said *Lual'* or *Deng* or *Wiu,* she would have been talking about the lesser gods, who when lumped together are called *Kuth,* the plural form of *Kuoth.* Anyone of the *Kuth* is referred to as *Kuoth,* so one is never sure which God the person is talking about, unless, as I said above, the person indicates his or her god by its own name. *Lual* and *Deng* are snakes and *Wiu* is a spear formerly belonging to a famous prophet. These are the greatest of the lesser gods, all of whom are very powerful and whom the people fear and appease.

I began to learn of the power of these gods and the taboos associated with them early in my African experience.

As I was studying language on the veranda, I heard a man calling from the other side of the house. The voice was loud and insistent, and not too different from any voice you heard daily at the door. I got up to see what he wanted.

"Tall girl," he said, urgently, "bring your gun." The word for "gun" was the noun *fire.*

"What is it?" I said.

"Snake!" he answered excitedly. Now he was peering through the screen at me. He was an older man, his head was shaved clean, and he wore a torn piece of old cloth, like a skirt, around his waist. He was one of the mission garden workers.

I got my gun, a .22 rifle, and followed the man to the peanut patch where he and another man were hoeing.

"What kind is it?" I said.

"It is *Deng*," he said. A short, thick, sluggish snake, which puffed itself out when irritated and did not move unless disturbed. It was poisonous and left unharmed by the Nuer because it was God; still, they hated it because of its bite and resulting wound, which very often ended with the loss of a foot or hand, and at times, death. Since the majority of snakes in the Sudan are deadly poisonous, and since death so plagued the people, it may not prove difficult to understand how the snake came to be God's main representative, or stand-in. The people were glad if snakes were killed, providing they did not have to do it.

So, in the peanut patch, just as the man said, I found the snake coiled and waiting.

"There it is," the other man said, and pointed at it with his hoe handle. "There. There," he repeated, making sure I saw it, while he himself stood back at a safe distance.

"Kill it. Kill it," the first man said. It took no skill to put the rifle to the snake's head, pull the trigger, and kill it. It was then robbed of its life, but not of its power. For truth had two sides that day, each mutually exclusive. It had two defendants. On one side, two virile men. Myself on the other. The men's side claimed that this snake was God, which, for them to kill, would bring God's wrath upon them. My side declared that the snake was a part of creation over which God had given man dominion. I was floored at the paradoxical thinking, which would condone and sponsor the killing of the object that represented God to them. It was ridiculous and indecent. With exasperation typical of my early days in that land, exciting my spirit into unbounded frustration aggravated by the inability to express myself adequately as yet, I sputtered forth an argument in an attempt to point out to them what to me was blatantly clear.

"You say this snake is God?"

"*Uh,* it is God."

"Then I have killed your God?"

The answer should have been yes, and I should have been able to say, "But how can this be? Can a person who is less than God kill God?" And they should have been able to see this (I wanted to think, anyway) and reply with relief, "Of course not." This is ridiculous. What fools we are; why haven't we seen this before? But instead of this they answered, "We don't know." And when pressed to explain why then they feared this creature, they laughed and said, because it was the custom of their fathers.

When the question came to the disposal of the snake, neither man would touch it. Why? I asked. Because we will die, they replied.

Then it was that I realized it was only God Himself who had the right to say, "Come now and let us reason together. . . ." This was my first lesson in the study of the responsibility God has assumed for mankind. I learned slowly. I found myself constantly wanting to assume the responsibility for Him, but He never relinquished

His sovereignty to me. Jesus' words helped me. He said, "My Father worketh hitherto and I work. . . . I can of mine own self do nothing." If God did not work, neither could I.

On another occasion, a teacher who was a believer called me to the village. A red cobra, the *Lual,* had gone into his hut and he wanted it killed. I had my rifle, but to be double-armed I grabbed a spear which was leaning against the thatch.

"No, don't take that," the teacher protested. "Its owner would not agree."

I put it back. I had read that the spear was the extension of a Nuer man's right arm, and I had just crossed swords with that fact. Even as no man would kill a snake, neither would his spear. I was trespassing on spiritual ground.

Inside the hut the light was dim. I crouched by the oval doorway holding my gun in readiness. The teacher was beside me. "Where did it go? Did you see where it went?" I asked him.

"Behind those sacks," he said. The sacks were against the mud wall. Next to them was an old bed with no webbing and some clay pots on the floor nearby. I went up to the sacks and tried to see behind them, but it was too dark. The teacher moved one of the sacks away from the wall, and I caught sight of the thick back of the snake and fired at it. I hit it, but it slithered behind the next sack. It was too dark to see anything and I waited. The only light was a pie-shaped wedge coming in through the door behind me. I was alone; the teacher had gone out. I stood in the middle of the hut, watching and listening. A chicken squawked in front of me, somewhere between me and the wall. It was on a nest. The snake was coming. I watched for it with my gun pointed at the floor. Presently, I saw the copper-colored head and white, beady eye coming out from between the clay pots. It kept coming steadily in my direction, heading for the door behind me. A well cobra is fast and cunning. This one was hurt and not coming so fast, but it was no doubt angry. I didn't know what it might do, and I was afraid. The gun was swaying in my hand. I knew it was wisest to wait until I could not miss and then shoot. So I let it come within two feet of my shoes, fired into its head, and killed it.

From outside the teacher called, "Do it again. Do it again." I did, and then slung the snake out the door with the barrel of the gun. The people standing outside jumped back. A young woman ran nervously away. "Big *Lual*," the people kept saying as if addressing it. "It is dead."

"It is truly dead?" someone asked.

"*Uh*, it is truly dead," another person answered.

"A bad snake," somebody said in disgust.

It was a very solemn and serious occasion marked especially for me by an old woman—with wrinkled stomach, gray hair, no teeth—who came up with a handful of grain which she threw to the snake in an act of absolution, saying, "Here, God, take this."

The people's fear of death and of God was synonymous. At times this fear became acute. I could only pray and wait. And as I waited I learned how intense their fear could be. A woman had twins at the clinic and had not been well ever since. She told the doctor that the twins were wrestling with God, meaning that God wanted one of them for himself. The woman was afraid that if He did not win, that is, if the twins grew strong, God would take *her*. So one day when the doctor went to see the patient he found that the smallest twin was very ill, and both the man and his wife said not to try and save the baby but to save the mother instead. The baby died. The woman's condition improved immediately and she recovered.

Another time, a woman who was having a miscarriage came to the clinic. There was nothing else the matter with her, but her family believed she was going to die and kept telling her that. She did die. Afterward, her young brother worked himself up into such a frenzy that he could not stand up by himself, and was groaning so loudly he could not talk. I saw him as the procession with the woman's body went past my house. I went out to listen to what was going on. The boy had collapsed on the ground and was crying out that he was the last of the children in the family, that everyone else had died, and he was sure to be next!

A Nuer policeman who came by on his bike stopped to counsel with the young man. Don't be silly, fellow, he said in effect, you're a young man. You've just been given your marks. Give God His ox and everything will be all right.

It was into *this* that I had come, to step across tradition and interpose my spiritual alternatives. I learned slowly how impossible this was to do. One day I asked a man, whom I found sobbing beside the body of his dead wife, if he knew the God, Jesus.

The man looked at me in despair and said, "Who is He?"

I realized at once how helpless I was to answer him.

Whatever the degree of spiritual darkness among the people might be, my own frustration might have been lessened if I had known to begin with what the function of taboos is. As it was, I was considering the nature of life and of God from a different set of facts from those the people used. Keeping taboos, I decided, gave men a security before God. Breaking them provided men with a reason for failure and death. Like going to the doctor did for me. When anyone wanted to know the cause of trouble, death for example, he could ultimately trace it to a broken taboo, for which, the people reasoned, God had brought punishment. Therefore, since it was God who killed people, a certain guarantee accompanied the keeping of taboos.

If I had been thinking straight, I would have had to ask myself some questions:

Is my scientific orientation to life, which has removed me from the constant threat of death, the factor which stabilizes my faith? Or, in that I need not fear God physically as the heathen do, has this freedom set me adrift from God, missing Him altogether?

And, is not the people's fear of God, which causes them to set up roadblocks in His path, and earns for them the designation "heathen," a more creditable indication of their acknowledgment of God than the American could-not-care-less attitude toward Him?

Is our understanding of God and the nature of God less culturally conditioned than that of the heathen?

Who in truth are the heathen?

I thought I knew.

Because of the indifference of the people to the Gospel, it was encouraging to recognize in Kuac a growing desire to read and discuss the Scripture. It seemed perfectly in order to anticipate that God had singled him out to be the messenger of the Gospel to his own people. However, when I first knew Kuac, he had yet to eat an egg. But the miracle occurred and the fear of death released its grip and, one by one, Kuac began to see the futility of taboos and to challenge his people. I remember spending a weekend with a small group of young men for the purpose of studying the Scripture. We had gone down the road in the Jeep and camped along the river under some thorn trees. One afternoon, a young man came walking along the road carrying a chicken. He stopped to look at us and Kuac immediately began to talk with him.

He asked the stranger his name and his village. The boy told him and then asked what we were doing there. Kuac explained that we were people of Jesus and we had come there to visit together. Then he asked the boy what he was doing with the chicken. "We are going to sacrifice it," the boy said. Kuac challenged him and asked him what the result of it would be. Had they not all sacrificed and was their life improved? No. "So why do you follow this talk, too?"

The boy looked at him with disapproval. "Your talk is the talk of the foreigner, and the automobile," he said, using the Arabic word for car. "It is not the talk of the people." Then he turned and went on his way.

This new set of ideas separated Kuac culturally from his people but drew him into a warm fellowship with the missionaries. Freed to live without fear of imminent death due to the breaking of taboos, Kuac lived confidently, expectantly, eager to try the foreigner's ways, and to do what they did. Life became a revelation to him; death was pushed further out of the way.

He no longer had ready explanations for why death occurred, and he had to rely on the white man to supply the scientific answers to death. But he was freed from the fear of it. He had now to find a way to reconcile death and the evils of the world with the love of God.

6

FROM BEADS TO BOOKS

Kuac went away to government school in a pair of old shorts and a borrowed shirt, and came back wearing a new khaki uniform which needed not only to be washed but ironed. So he would borrow our charcoal iron. To buy his own would be too expensive.

His beads and bracelets were gone. He combed his hair into a springy mat. He had acquired foreign tastes. He liked onions, vegetable oil, and tea with sugar, and to complete his outfit, he had acquired a pair of leather shoes and socks. They were the first pair of leather shoes he had ever had. He got them in Malakal and I remember looking at them and thinking, Will he keep them tied and clean? He did. He had those shoes for years.

He spoke English much better now and he owned a few books. I made him a table out of packing boxes and painted it green. This, an old chair, and a rickety Arab-style bed—leather strips woven to a wooden frame on legs—were his modern possessions.

He had no source of income. The economy of the tribe was not based on income. What money he had he "found," as the Nuer say, which meant he asked it of someone else. No one claimed permanent possession of anything, least of all money. A wife, the most valuable possession a man could have, was recognized as family property and called "ours" by the male members of the husband's clan, since she had been paid for by communal cattle, but the husband retained the right to sleep with her.

Beads, bracelets, cloths, grain were passed around within the clan. Money, which was a less-needed commodity, was treated the same way. It could be asked for without incurring any obligation to pay it back. Only cattle could not be asked for in this way, because in many ways cattle shared the same status as people. This asking for something for nothing had its own word in the language. It contained an element of begging but did not carry with it the stigma of poverty. It embraced a much larger concept of give-and-take.

It was difficult to express the idea of borrowing and lending. You could say, "Give me this; I will return it." But to say, "Neither a borrower nor a lender be" was impossible because these were not separate concepts.

The system was fair because every giver was a potential receiver since he was as free to ask of another as he was obligated to give.

The need to ask was waived at times. For this reason, stealing, as Americans understand it, was of little consequence to the people. They seldom used the word in connection with the disappearance of another's possession. A house might be broken into and the grain in it stolen, but the owners preferred to say, "It was taken." Houseboys thought nothing of taking sugar, matches, or kerosene from the white man's house, but became furious if they were accused of stealing anything. A young man whom I knew well, and who was accustomed to the white man's ways, asked me one day to buy him a wristwatch in Khartoum. "But you have a wristwatch," I said. "What happened to it?"

"It was taken by a friend of mine," he said.

"Stolen, you mean?" I said, and he laughed.

The purest use of the word *steal* occurred when a girl, for whom a down payment of cattle had been paid, outwitted her family and would-be husband, and ran away with the man she desired. Of this girl it was said, "She stole herself." The consequence of such an act often led to clan warfare and murder.

It remained a mystery to the majority of the people why we missionaries did not share our possessions with them. We claimed to be their friends. We said God was their friend. We made a translation of the song, "There's Not a Friend Like the Lowly Jesus." But the people wondered why we did not act like friends. The reason for the confusion was that their idea of a friend was different from ours. We often used the word freely when speaking to or about somebody, and on occasion we were told not to use it that way, but it was a long time before I understood why.

One day a man in a green felt hat, wearing blue beads at his neck and a white plastic belt around his middle and nothing else, stood outside my house, with a wooden walking stick in his hand, calling my name.

I went to the door and, recognizing him, let him in. He had not been to my house before and I was surprised to see him. He was a villager whom I had come to know when his brother, who had been badly mauled by a lion, was a patient at the clinic. I had often visited him, and on those visits had talked with Riak, too. I was living away from Nasir at the time, at Ler on the west bank of the Nile, and I knew only a few people and thought of Riak as my friend.

There was an odd assortment of chairs on the veranda, and Riak decided upon the green deck chair with the wide arms and the orange-and-white-striped canvas. He negotiated it easily, grasping the ends of the arm rests with his hands and sinking down into the canvas, his head not quite reaching the upper wooden roller, but his hat going on up and sticking out over the top. The back of the chair was pushed up as straight as it would go, and he had his feet back against the rung, which brought his knees up somewhere in the vicinity of his chest. On his face was a self-satisfied smile.

I sat down in a straight-backed chair against the limed wall, looked at Riak, and wished that the monotony of *my* routine could be broken by something as simple as a chair.

Riak began the conversation by inquiring about Jumo Kenyatta, whom, of course, he did not know; but the casual way in which he spoke about him, referring to him only as Jumo, gave me the feeling that he had known him all his life. The truth was he had got all of his information through young schoolboys. I exhausted my information rather quickly and after that there was a period of relaxed silence, and then Riak cocked his head to one side and said, "Nyarial, I want you to be my friend." Well, that was a nice thing to say, I thought, but I anticipated that this was a leading remark to be followed by some colossal request. So I said, "It is good," meaning, Go on, what else?

And he said, "Nyarial, you will give me a cow and I will be your friend. And then it will be said by everyone, 'This cow was given to Riak by Nyarial. She is a chief. Nyarial is Riak's friend.'"

I found it difficult to resist the eager smile, but neither was I about to give him a cow. If I were to give him a cow, as soon as the gift were noised abroad, then everyone would want me to be his friend. But I was learning what it meant to be a friend. It was being admitted to the inner circle, becoming part of the family, literally gaining the status of a relative, and the rights and privileges of the clan.

"If there is no cow, can we not still be friends?" I said.

He smiled, and we laughed and somehow we both knew, No, we could not be "friends."

Kuac became a friend without the cow, but we gave him a good lantern, a pressure lamp, a charcoal iron, taught him how to drive the motorboat, how to do simple carpentry, and gave him some new tools. He even learned how to knit and made himself a sleeveless sweater in red and blue yarn. However, the more he had the more he wanted. He was no longer content to eat his meals from a gourd on the floor, so he wanted a table for which he needed chairs and proper bowls and spoons. He needed glasses for tea and a primus stove and a teapot and kerosene for the stove. This was all a part of progress, which was encouraging to us and was even looked upon as divine blessing because he was emerging from heathenism, his mind was grasping new things. However, his basic concept of economics remained unchanged. He had no understanding of the responsibility of a money economy, and in the end this proved disastrous.

Kuac was climbing up the social and spiritual ladder of the mission quite well. It was a genuine climb, unaffected by airs of any kind which so often accompanied this phenomenon on mission stations. He looked and acted more like the white man, but at the same time he remained loyal to his family and his people. He did not divorce himself from them; he did not want to. He was proud of the fact that he was a Nuer. But he was now engaged in a battle, waging his own little war against the tribal customs, carrying on what he had learned from the missionaries with convictions he now claimed as his own. There was not a little valor connected with this because the Christian way of life and thought was devastating to that which the Nuer espoused. To have once been a part of it, and then to pioneer against it, was dangerous for a young man to do. He would be the logical one to blame for any disaster striking the family or village or clan.

When his mother, who had listened charitably to his Christian teaching, became ill and threatened to die, Kuac was home on school holiday. There was something in her stomach, she thought; a foreign object which would have to come out so that she would not die. The only person who could get it out was a *tiet*. A *tiet* was an especially equipped person who, by sleight-of-hand, could produce in a very short time a stick, or a piece of broken pottery, or glass whenever necessary from another person's stomach, thereby relieving the person of whatever ailed him. The word *tiet* came from a verb meaning, "to grasp mentally."

Kuac remonstrated with his mother and urged her to leave that idea and trust only in God. He did not expect her to recover; it was important to him, though, that she die in the hands of God.

The old woman finally agreed, and no *tiet* came. She died, and Kuac kept vigil at the hut until her burial, forbidding any women to mourn. Mourning was a device to ward off the contagion of death.

I do not know what happened in Kuac's family to affect their trend toward Christianity, nor do I know the extent of their comprehension of what Christianity was, but eventually both of Kuac's brothers and their wives and his sister's old husband were baptized. For anyone professing Christianity his attitude at death or in the face of death was the big test. If, when confronted with death or the possibility of death, a man affirmed allegiance to Jesus, or negatively, if he did not succumb in fear and resort to calling on a heathen god, it was noteworthy. When Buoy, the old husband of Kuac's sister, was sick and close to death, Kuac and I went to his hut to see him. It was a Sunday morning and the old man lay on his sleeping skin, covered with a grimy cloth, almost too weak to talk.

We sat down beside him and Kuac said to him, "Buoy, I am Kuac, do you know me?"

The old man's eyes flickered, opened, and looked for a moment, and then his mouth began to move. At first there was no voice, and then it came and we heard, "It is you, Kuac?" Then he moved his arm and touched Kuac on the knee, feeling him, and tried to speak again, but began to cough, and he turned his head and tried to spit on the ground. Finally he said, "Kuac." And Kuac said, "*Uh.*" And he said, "My child," and there was a pause, then, "I am dying," and another pause, and then, "I go to Jesus." Then, summoning all of his strength it seemed, he lifted his frail right arm, and as he did so, Kuac bent his head down, and the old man touched his fingers on Kuac's head, thereby passing to the child the life of the elder. It was a great thing for the old man to do. His wife did not like it and refused to allow either Kuac or me back into her hut. She was apparently jealous or furious that her husband had bypassed her. She also let it be known that she did not appreciate his reference to Jesus.

Kuac continued to be the bright spot in our missionary endeavor. He was almost becoming Exhibit A. In my experience at the mission he was the first African who could lead a church service and do it well. By that I mean he had the poise of someone who has something to say and knows how to say it. To him the Word of God said something, and aided by his natural ability to teach he turned a Sunday meeting into a thing desirable. I can remember on one occasion his saying to the people, "What is the oil of this world?"— using the word meaning butter oil, the richest food the people had.

An old man on the bench in front of him answered, "The hearts of men."

"Yes, it is so," Kuac said, "just as a woman looks and looks for the oil to appear while she's churning, so God looks and looks for the hearts of men that He might make them for Himself."

Kuac also liked to go with us to the cattle camps in the dry season to preach to the people there. These camps were along the rivers, and grew up in the dry season when the people left their villages, which were always made on the highest possible rise of ground for what protection could be had against the annual inundation of river water and hence were not near the swamps where the grass remained green for much of the dry season. The camps were an amalgamation, usually quite large, of people, and in terms of Western efficiency, provided for the missionary an ideal situation for "reaching" people with the Gospel. The idea of going out and preaching was not a revelation of God to Kuac; he learned it from us missionaries. He only went when we went. But this encouraged us to believe that he was eager for his people to hear the Gospel and led us to expect greater evidences of devotion from him in the future.

Our coming to the cattle camps provided entertainment for the villagers in that they not only heard a new story, but could also investigate the white people and their clothes and skin and hair, and whatever else they could put their hands on. The spiritual value of the trips was never realized in numbers turning from heathenism to Christianity, but was part of the continual revelation, to me at least, of the well-knit society in which these people lived, and the strength of it, from which they had no desire or reason to turn.

I would return home from these trips disheartened by our lack of progress, and searching within why it was that God did not give His Word entrance to the people's hearts. Whether it was merely the novelty of riding and driving a motorboat, or the enjoyment of an easy journey, or whether he had some real reason to hope, of which I was unaware, I do not know, but Kuac was never discouraged at the lack of response from his people. He was never appalled, as I was, by their ways, and he maintained that, as a people, they sought for God.

7

A PURCHASED POSSESSION

The world of education was new and bewildering to young Africans. Far and above a thirst for knowledge was a thirst for status, which only the schools could give. To be able to say one was in school, or had been to school, whether he had completed his course, failed his course, or had left it uncompleted, gave one social prominence at any age. A school certificate usually meant a job; and a job meant a place on the government's wage escalator where one's salary increased periodically according to varying scales.

Money was especially valuable because it could be converted into cattle, enabling a man to have more than one wife, which was his goal and the standard by which young men judged each other's progress.

I had an armchair, which had been made in Khartoum of cheap, light-grained wood, that I had bought from a Nuer man for about eighteen dollars. The man had the distinction of being a member of the original Legislative Assembly, the first governing body of the new, independent Sudan. After the first coup by the army the members returned to their homes throughout the country, and this man, who had formerly been a teacher and who lived in a modified mud hut, brought back a chair which he had had in Khartoum as part of his domestic furnishings, and asked me to buy it, because, he said, "I want to buy a cow."

When Kuac finished at the government school he had to decide between a bright financial future or working at the mission. He had always said that he wanted to "do the work of God," which was a term used by prophets and sorcerers to explain what they did; but Kuac was using it in the Christian sense of preaching to his people.

He was approached by a British official in the Ministry of Education at Malakal who offered him a job, hopefully wooing him by saying that his record of honesty in the school made him highly desirable. Kuac, however, was wary of the government in those days because of agitation in the country for independence. Whatever happened, he felt his future in the government's service would be insecure.

He came home to ask his family what he should do. It was they who confirmed that he should "do the work of God," perhaps because both the work of God and that of the white man were synonymous to them. For Kuac to be employed by the mission, or at least to be in its care, assured them of a source of income which would make grain, sugar, cloth, cattle, beads, blankets, mosquito nets, and whatever money could buy available to them. They were totally resigned to the status quo, which in faraway Nasir was yet undisturbed, and they failed to anticipate the imminent evictions of the missionaries.

By January 1, 1956, the Sudan had become independent. Immediately the new Arab government in Khartoum began a campaign to "Sudanize" every possible foreign-held job with Sudanese citizens. Anticipating this, the mission had taken steps to become affiliated with the Bishop Gwynne College, an Anglican divinity school located in Equatoria Province, at Maridi near the Congo border. An institution of the British Church Missionary Society, it was the only Protestant training school for clergymen in the Sudan and was primarily for southerners. It was later to be destroyed by fire in the civil war which came between the southerners and the Arabs. According to the plan of cooperation established by the two participating missions, the Reform doctrine was to be taught by ordained missionary teachers supplied by the American Mission.

In an effort to prepare southerners as pastors and church leaders, the mission hunted for young men in the four tribes among whom it worked to send to the divinity school. Their search was restricted to a very small group of schoolboys, who, to qualify, read and spoke English well. Of the baptized men among the Nuer, only

Kuac and another man were interested. Encouraged by the popular trend to go to school, and guided by his earliest desire to do the work of God and the confirmation of his family as well, Kuac agreed to attend the divinity college, and of the two Nuer men ever to be enrolled, was the only one to finish.

The work of the church, or in this case, the mission, does not guarantee the working of God, for in spite of men's attempts, the working of God cannot be definitely graphed or exclusively charted. Depending upon its brand of theology, a mission defines its goals. In the American Mission the ultimate goal was to establish churches pastored by Africans. The Reform doctrine of the mission dictated how this would be done. In America, if one disagreed with the doctrine of a particular church he was free to leave it and choose another; but in this land, a man like Kuac had no choice in the matter. He took in good faith the leading of the missionaries into whose hands destiny had placed him without benefit of alternatives. If the church was to survive, the mission said, there must be organized congregations and ordained pastors. These congregations, it was predetermined, would be answerable to a court called the Presbytery. It would be connected by a lifeline to the United Presbyterian Church of the USA in New York City. Impetus, ideas, vision, finances would come from New York through the Presbytery until the African pastors caught on to managing things themselves, which few ever doubted would come to pass.

The validity of such an arrangement was not questioned, and the pitfalls were never explored or explained to the people. The basic idea was a product of Reform doctrine, and what was good for Calvin was certainly good for the south Sudan. Whether or not John Calvin would have reached the conclusions he did had he first been exposed to primitive heathenism, no one questioned.

When Kuac entered the school he had had very little contact with the outside world. He had not been out of the province, nor had he ever seen a train, multistoried buildings, or the cinema. Flying across the Mediterranean Sea that year on my way home on furlough, I wrote to him, commenting on the flight and explaining how I had just had my dinner. He replied to this:

"I was very happy with your letter which reached me. You were writing it the same time you were running in the sky canoe. The sky canoe is surely a good thing when a person can be writing in it while running with it. Did your head not go round in circles? I was very perplexed at this. Probably it is because I have never traveled in a sky canoe which makes me so perplexed."

Kuac was slow to adapt to the new surroundings at the school. It was in a strange part of the country; the soil was red and stony, the land was hilly, and outcroppings of rock stuck up menacingly into the sky. The river near the school was only a small stream and had no fish, and there were no cattle grazing on the slopes. For Kuac this was untenable. His schoolmates, most of whom were from this area, were short and heavy-set, were hunters not cattlemen, used bow and arrow instead of spears, and did not build barns.

He was not happy with the masters in the school, either. With characteristic frankness and a twinge of bitterness, prompted by the growing, popular attitude among the Arabs and educated Africans to consider the white man, and particularly the British, with scorn; and misjudging the natural reserve of the English, comparing them with Americans, interpreting their failure to communicate thoughts and feelings as deliberate unkindness, he wrote me a letter.

"These white people here," he wrote, "teach us what Jesus said, yet they are still despising the African students. Remember, love hides nothing from its friend."

His masters dealt patiently with him and at the end of the school year he wrote again to me. The letter was in English.

"I am very glad to let you know that if God wills it I will come back to this school next year in spite of difficulties of this year. And for next year I must bear the burden of responsibility of better study in the book of Christ Jesus than this year."

His next letter was written the same year, following a trip he had made with his friend Gac Rik and a missionary. The purpose of the trip was to visit an area there where a spiritual movement had been going on for many years.

In this letter, which he wrote entirely in English, he attempts to explain missionaries' behavior in spiritual terms: "I have seen things in them binding them up, such as their customs; for example, their custom of being proud that they are the ruling class and [proud] of their environment which are not at all agreed with the life of Christ, for if there is no guidance of the Holy Spirit many actions may not be from the Lord, as I suppose."

Facing the practice of public confession of sin which he saw demonstrated in Ruanda, he wrote in the next paragraph, in obscure English, that for himself he realized he only repented of his sins before Christ because "I do not see Him like men who can despise me and send me away from work." This was a confession of his own fear of the mission policy that sin must not be condoned, and such sins as were especially frowned upon by the missionaries frequently resulted in the defendant's dismissal, if he happened to be in the mission employ. This unique situation ensured that censure would always rest in the hands of the white man; that sins of the missionaries, visible of course to the Africans, would never be treated equally. I had another letter from Kuac many years later, in which he wrote of a situation involving himself and two other missionaries, and of the attitude of one of the missionary's he said, "How can it be that Christians can malign each other like that?"

It was while Kuac was in the divinity school, his second year there, that he came to me one day while home on holiday and said, "I am going to marry." I was not surprised but wondered how he would negotiate a heathen marriage.

"Whom will you marry?" I said. "Have you picked a girl?"

"*Uh*," he said, "it is a person of our village."

"What is her name?"

"She is called Nyatiac."

"Does she agree to you?" I said.

"*Uh*, she agrees to me." He smiled.

"You have found the girl, now only the cattle remain to be found. Is it not so?"

"*Uh.*" He laughed.

"To marry" literally meant "to count" and referred to the counting of the available cattle a man will give to a family in return for their daughter. The minimum price, fixed by the government, was twenty head of cattle—an assortment of cows, bulls, calves, and steers. Not all Nuer were satisfied with this price and in some cases demanded more.

Marriage was not determined by love, but by a series of agreements. If a man brought "marriage talk" to a girl, she sent the "word of agreement" back to him by her friends if this was her pleasure. Following this, in order for the marriage transaction to be made, there had to be agreement between the two families concerning the cattle. If the families could not agree, the transaction was dropped and there was no marriage.

Seldom did a young man have sufficient cattle in his family for immediate payment, so the woman's family decided to agree or disagree on the basis of the number and quality of the animals available and whether or not there was a good prospect of future payments.

In the meantime a down payment of one animal is taken to the barn of the girl's family as an announcement that this girl is spoken for.

"Did you take your cow?" I asked Kuac.

"No, not yet. It will be taken in these days."

"Have you talked, you and her people?"

"*Uh,* we have talked."

"Did they agree to you?"

"*Uh,* they agreed to me. They want the cattle. The girl's brothers want to marry."

"What kind of a girl is their sister?"

"She is a good girl. She does the cooking for the family, for her father and her brothers. Their mother is dead. The girl is the only one who is there."

"Is she a young girl?"

"*Uh,* she is small."

"Is she a person who believes God?"

"Oh, I don't know. She is a young girl."

"Do you know their God?"

"I think their God is *Lual.*"

"Have you talked to the girl?"

"*Uh,* I have talked a little with her. I have not talked much with her. We must pray that she will become a Christian."

A few years before I would have panicked at this. But as it was there simply were no Christian girls, and God, I thought, would not hold a man responsible.

"When will you have the dance?"

"It is not yet. I have not got my cows. Perhaps it will be done next year."

The dance was a communal affair attended by members of the two participating clans. Unlike other Nilotic tribes, of which the Nuer people were the second in size, numbering over three hundred and fifty thousand, the Nuer confined themselves to one major dance, the marriage dance. This dance was called *bul,* which meant "drum."

Always held in the dry season when the ground was hard, the dance was announced early in the morning by the steady, pulsating rhythm of the drum beating out its message across the otherwise silent plain. The young people prepared themselves, oiling their black bodies, shining their bracelets, coloring their faces with blotches of brick dust or chalk. The slender young girls, whose daily attire was beads and bracelets, put on their dancing skirts made of thin strands of braided grass about twelve inches long, tied to a band.

The young men had begun their preparations some days before. Having let their hair grow long they made a paste out of soft cow-dung ash and water, smearing it onto the hair to form it into a peak which they brought to the front over their foreheads. The paste hardened into a crust, and in the process the kinky hair was straightened and its blackness bleached into strawberry blond. After the ashes were washed away and the hair dried and shaken out, what then appeared resembled a tinted dandelion down.

Some wore a *thiaw,* which is a series of thin metal bracelets, encasing the left arm from elbow to wrist, causing the hand to swell. A young man who could obtain it had a large ivory band on his right thumb with which to stroke the bracelets on his arm. This made a noise that pleased him.

Giraffe-tail necklaces were highly prized. Men would drive a giraffe into a mud bog and cut off its tail. This long, black, wiry hair they made into many-stranded necklaces which they wore at dances, one on top of the other until a man's neck was full.

Middle-aged women bedecked themselves in strange assortments of available clothing, plumed their hair with ostrich feathers, and brandished fly switches in the air.

On the morning of the dance, the groom and his male attendant, wearing leopard-skin loincloths to distinguish them, toured the area on foot at a steady canter, holding their spears aloft, running and jumping one behind the other in unison, chanting a ballad of the marriage as they ran.

At midday, parties of young men grouped according to age sets snaked their way in similar manner to the dance, running, jumping, chanting as they ran, following the path through the villages under the open sky and the burning sun.

The girls ran to the dance in bunches, some with tassled sticks, to arrange themselves in receiving lines for the men. After arriving, the men would circle the drums, chanting loudly above the beat, then break away from the center and snake their way to the girls. The girls, standing erect, with their arms held in front of them in a horse-driving position, were almost motionless except for the concerted up-and-down movement of their buttocks, which bounced the cow-tail pompoms on the tops of their dancing skirts.

The men, facing them, no longer sang, but kept up a brisk tramping motion with their feet, holding their spears in their right hands like flags. Both sides looked straight ahead; not a glimmer of recognition crossed their sober faces. Suddenly the men would break away and continue to dance—to jump and to chant and to circle the drums. Couples of male dancers teamed up to fight mock battles, going at each other with their spears poised, ramming them at each other in play, dodging the blades with quick side maneuvers.

As the air filled with clouds of dust, and the din of singing voices and beating drums rolled across the plain, the business of the marriage went on inside the barn. Elders from both families met in a solemn conference. Sitting on the floor, the men with their legs drawn up and crossed in front of them, the women with their legs stretched straight out or tucked neatly under them, they deliberated over the cattle. Before them on the floor lay a pile of straws representing the available cattle payment. Backs bending, as if engrossed in a game of pick-up sticks, they debated each animal's record. They argued the quality of each straw, calling it by the name of the animal it represented. If it were a cow, they knew how many times it had calved and how many of its offspring were heifers and how many bulls. They knew the age of each animal, the history of ownership, and its progeny. They knew how the animals came to belong to this family, whether by birth or in payment of a debt, or through marriage or a money purchase.

In such a gathering, women speak as well as men. Each tries to get the best of the bargain, for the cattle are apportioned to several leading members of the family, such as the father's eldest sister and the mother's eldest brother.

If the families cannot agree and the marriage is canceled, it is said, *Ci bul dak,* which means literally, "The dance fell apart."

In my house on the day that Kuac told me, "I am going to marry," I said to him, "How will you get the cattle?"

And he answered, "I have a plan."

It was expedient that Kuac have a plan, since he was a product of the mission, training for the ministry. He could not do as his younger brother had done, who, when faced with this dilemma of insufficient cattle, took a girl he wanted for his wife and fathered her child. He then set about to earn money to buy cattle to pay for her. This was common practice, sanctioned by the people, whose reaction was tempered by the knowledge that if men were to refrain from marriage until sufficient cattle were at hand, few of them would ever marry. This predicament did not precipitate the abolishment of the cattle system. Instead, the people reveled in its complexities, spent their lives discussing cattle, forever hopeful of "finding" a cow. Theirs was not a frustrated existence; it was serene—a company, knit together, of men, women, children, and cattle.

It was a woman's glory and security to be purchased with cattle. She knew herself as someone of worth. There was nothing more valuable to the Nuer than their cattle. On a certain day, some years

after their marriage, I was riding with Nyatiac, Kuac's wife, as we passed a herd of cattle grazing near the road. She cried out to me, "*Ah,* Nyarial, look! There is a cow like the one of my marriage." And she named it by its markings, her face alight with joy.

The plan which Kuac mentioned to me that day he wrote later in a letter while I was away in Malakal. It was written in ink on copy-book paper, with a clear, masculine hand, and it read:

Dear Nyarial:

If you agree to it, you may think about this plan. If it is a good plan, tell me. If you agree to it I will praise our Lord and honor Him for this good plan.

I know that if the Lord has not said that there will be money available, nobody can bring it forth; and if no one agrees to bring his money when God tells him, God will not force him. But how can we know that God has prepared our hearts to give money, or that He has not prepared them? That is the talk of each man, alone.

This is my plan which I think is a good one, but maybe it is not a good one, too: The buying of cattle is difficult. The cattle which I told you about before are very many, and you shall not search for them all. But if you are able for the buying of five cows, buy them. The nine or ten other cows which I spoke of, leave them.

I have four cows now, and my brother's two cows [which he had bought for payment of his own wife] will be included.

[Then he wrote in English]:

As you are interested in buying these five cows for me I will not even borrow much money. I will borrow only fifteen pounds to enable me to have six cows plus your five, equals eleven cows. Other friends and relatives will give the other four cows to make the Christians pay their expected number. [Then he resumed in Nuer]:

If you want those cattle to be bought in Malakal, it is good talk. But tell me so that I can send a person on this boat leaving Nasir, to bring those cattle back on foot.

Is it not good that you will tell me the amount of money that you find, so that I can know the amount of money I must search for? [Again in English he wrote]:

If I ask evilly please forgive me. "Be kindly affectioned one to another with brotherly love, in honor preferring one another; not slothful in business, fervent in spirit, serving the Lord. Rejoicing in hope; patient in tribulation; continuing instant in prayer; distributing to the necessity of saints." [Romans 12:10–13.] Be kind to me. Do what you feel the Lord wants you to do.

"Is it not to deal thy bread to the hungry, and that thou bring the poor that are cast out to thy house? When thou seest the naked, that thou cover him, and that thou hide not thyself from thine own flesh?" [Isaiah 58:7.]

The question is urgent. I want to know something about it and do something else before August, but it is not a sorrowful and shameful thing, my sister, perhaps we shall glorify God in it.

I know I talk with you about physical need, but I know it pleases God as my faith and hope in Christ stand firm; the Lord will not be pleased if He sees my faith fails. God is love; He judges lovingly and wisely.

[Again in Nuer he wrote], If you honestly think it is not good talk, tell me. My heart is happy with you, my sister.

> Your friend in Christ,
> Kuac Nyoat

The mission had declared a Nuer marriage incomplete and hence sinful if sufficient cattle had not been paid. It seemed to me that if a man was unable to pay for the cattle, he had only one alternative: to trust God for the money. This idea was more teachable than believable. It meant that one must be able to believe God would rain down cows out of heaven, and this I was not able to believe. Thus by our teaching, we forced ourselves into becoming God for Kuac and gave him the money to buy five cattle. Fortunately for us, no other men married on his plan.

8

TRAINING A WIFE

Kuac's treatment of his young wife pursued the course he had set for himself. After the marriage dance (which he did not attend) and the *mut*—the act which separates the girl from her family, when her head is shaved, her beads and bracelets are removed, and she puts on the beads and decorations from her husband, and the loincloth which marks her as a woman—after this happened, instead of following custom and allowing his wife to remain at home until the first child is born, Kuac brought Nyatiac to his own house at the mission.

The structure of the house was foreign to Nyatiac. It was a rectangular building of mud and sticks and thatch, divided into three sections by mud walls. Each room had a square window covered with screening, and the center section had a tall, wooden door painted green. The ceiling of the house was thatch. In one end-room was Kuac's Arab-style bed, a table and chair, his metal boxes and books, and his bicycle. Above the bed was a grass rope strung with his clothes hung across it, and on the table, which was by the window, was a pressure lantern, a flashlight, and an array of books and papers. The center section, which had two child's-size metal chairs with the grass webbing worn through, was very narrow but was usually full of people sitting on the chairs and on the bumpy mud floor. The third room was very dark and was where the sacks of grain and odds and ends were kept.

The door of the house was huge, the size of door used in a foreigner's house, and was in the wall of the center section and let in a lot of light, a lot of air, and many flies and mosquitoes.

Nyatiac had not worn clothes before. When she was a girl clothes were not required. Now, as Kuac's wife, he bought her cotton prints and plastic sandals. Kuac washed her clothes when he washed his own because he knew how to wash clothes and he was afraid she would not take care of the soap properly. Most people were careless with soap, letting it melt away in the water and when they did not have any more, the clothes they had did not get washed.

Under her dress Nyatiac wore muslin underpants, which took the place of the loincloth all women wore, and clothed in these alone she would cook in front of her house, wearing the dress and sandals only when she went to the clinic, to the merchants, or to church.

She still cooked on an open fire, on the ground, using sticks or cornstalks for fuel, but instead of gourds to eat from, Kuac bought enamel bowls from the local merchants, with blue and red and yellow designs, which were made in Czechoslovakia. He also got for her a large aluminum tray and thin aluminum pots. Kuac made a table with boards he got from the mission, because there was nowhere else he could get boards or nails, and Nyatiac kept all of her cooking utensils on this table outside in the sun, where they would dry after she had washed them at the river. She learned to cook with oil and to make tea with sugar and mint. She also learned to make *kisera* like the Arabs, to fold it and put it on the aluminum tray around the enamel bowl of meat and onion stew.

She did not like this way of living at first and threatened to go back to the village. Kuac worried about this and wondered what to do. He did not want to beat her, even though she expected this, as every woman did, but he did not know how to accomplish the disciplining a good beating might do. He knew how the women thought, that if a wife wasn't beaten occasionally she began to worry that she had lost favor in her husband's sight, that he did not care about having her around any more. It was an effective custom in a culture where the people are largely undisciplined as children, but Kuac was influenced by the white man's concepts of love, and although he was tempted, he did not beat her. This left him with a dilemma.

"What shall I do?" he said to me.

"Respect her," I answered, "and be patient. Remember, she has her ideas, too. This way you have brought her makes no sense to her."

"I am a very hard man," he said. "Sometimes my talk is very strong. Ask God for me."

When I first met Nyatiac, the marriage had just been completed. She was predictably shy then, as a young married woman is. But within her was a fountain of laughter which could not be sealed. She would laugh when she could not find the courage to talk, and her laugh was a loud, merry, metallic laugh which she would embellish at the end with a flourish of her tongue. She was not as tall as most women, an inch or so shorter than Kuac, but her carriage was perfect, her breasts even and firm, her teeth beautifully straight and white. These were the physical qualities Nuer men desired.

She came to my Bible class, after she was married, and sat on the floor against the wall next to the bedroom. She came because Kuac told her to come. It was a part of her new life. Christianity was utterly foreign to her, but in the marriage agreement with her father and brothers, Kuac had stipulated that his God would now become Nyatiac's, and that she would now be under no further obligation to her father's gods. The men readily agreed to this because they were anxious to get the cattle Kuac had so that they themselves could marry.

For a long time Nyatiac sat like a scared rabbit, not saying a word. Weeks went by before her shyness wore away and she began to laugh, then to talk, and eventually to sing. But she would never commit herself if asked a question about the lesson, or about the Bible, preferring to appear dumb rather than to speak and be mistaken.

She attended Kuac's class for communicants, and she learned to read before her first child was born, and in time she was baptized. These things were all a part of her marriage; she also began to braid her hair like the Arabs.

The stuff of which she was made showed up later, when Kuac was imprisoned by the local government, accused of abetting a plot against them. Arab soldiers in army trucks went through the villages near the mission, frightening the people late at night. Soldiers went to Nyatiac's house and took her away for interrogation before the officers. She was petrified with fear, imagining what they might do to Kuac. She was led out of the darkness into a room blazing with light and told to stand before the officers. The officers told her lies. They said Kuac had confessed to being in the house of the *mamur*, a local official, when the infamous meeting took place; they wanted to know if this was true. Tell us the truth, they said. If you lie, Kuac will be punished.

"Chief," she said, "even if you say you will kill Kuac I cannot say this is true."

They let her go, and Kuac was eventually released.

Women did not show a fondness for their husbands. Affection was given to the children. But Nyatiac had a guarded fondness for Kuac. She liked to be where he was. Her eyes followed him as he preached or spoke. They lit up proudly at the mention of his name. But she was also objective about him and she admitted to me one day how incapable he was of handling money. He trusted her and gave her money to buy food at the merchants. He should have given her the money to keep that he doled out to the relatives.

Nyatiac's first pregnancy was abortive. One morning Kuac came and said that Nyatiac was having her baby. We were not at Nasir then; we were far away, at Ler, on the west bank of the Nile, at a mission station there. Kuac and I were translating the letters of Peter.

"She is in much pain," he said. "When she is in pain, I am in pain. Come and see."

It was in the rainy season. Everything was green. The sun was out. The sky was blue. Great white clouds were floating around in it. We walked from the house, down the sandy lane, in the shade of the lacy-leaved poinciana trees, to the house with the cement walls and floor where Kuac and his wife were living. Any other young husband would not have dared to be present at this time lest, if his wife died, he might die, too.

Inside the open door Nyatiac was kneeling on the floor; her face was in an agony, bathed in tears and perspiration, but she was not crying audibly. She was waiting. Then rising on her knees, with her back straight and slightly forward, she bore down with the pain, gripping her thighs with her hands, her legs spread apart, and at the apex of the pain began to cry out: *Ayow! Ayow! Ayow!* until she could only catch her breath, squeeze her eyes shut, and grimace with the pain.

In a little while a fetus of two months was born. Some time later, when I had returned to my own house, Kuac came. "Nyarial," he said, "it is still"—meaning the unburied fetus was still in the house. "What shall I do?"

Do? I thought. What shall he do? For a moment I did not understand what he meant; then I did.

"We'll bury it," I said. "Will that not be good?"

"*Uh*," he said, relieved.

The difficulty was that only *people* were buried. Things were thrown away. A fetus was a thing. No baby was called a person until it was weeks old and the initial dangers were over. (The mortality rate in the first year of life was 50 percent.) When the child's life was established, it was recognized as a person and given a name. At birth, fear and sorrow ebbed and flowed, depending upon the mother's recovery. What happened to the baby was of little consequence in contrast, for in time another child would be born. This attitude forestalled any preparation for or anticipation of the new baby. It was a defense mechanism against disappointment, and an attempt to outwit God, for if the child was ignored, they thought, as not being a person, God would overlook it and it would live. But as surely as His attention was drawn to it, He would kill it.

Obviously, Kuac was seeing it all from another point of view.

So I got a matchbox, and we went together and dug a little grave, and buried it, and prayed, asking God for another child.

9

"PATHTOR MOTHETH"

The next year—1958—when the credulous villagers were killing sacrifices in a fearful recognition of the first U.S. satellite visible to them in the night sky, and the houseboys were asking what those "sky canoes" were you saw first and heard later, Kuac was ordained as the first pastor in the Nuer tribe. In him the missionaries placed their hope for a future Nuer church. Upon him they placed the responsibility. His picture appeared in the mission-printed magazine *Light,* together with the newly ordained pastor from the Shilluk tribe, both wearing white robes and in company with fellow-ordained missionaries. The article accompanying the picture rejoiced in what was taking place in the church in the south Sudan, and emphasized that these men belonged to Africa and the Africans, that they were *their* pastors and would need *their* support.

The day the mission had been waiting and praying for had at last arrived.

Kuac now walked among the people with a new name. He was called Pastor Moses Kuac. He had chosen the name Moses when he was in divinity school, reversing a decision he had made earlier in his life when he declared that he would always be called Kuac. However, he was now in a select group where foreign names replaced tribal names and where the title "Pastor" gave the members a new status among the foreigners and the educated African elite. But to the villagers, the name was both unpronounceable and meaningless except to identify Kuac with the foreigner. This it certainly did. To the African, names are very important. They are the index of a person's life. Each person's name disclosed either an event or the family's attitude toward another person (usually the child's father), or toward God at the time of birth. Then, all males at the time of initiation received a bull's name, signifying their manhood and marking them as members of a particular age set. And finally, parents of grown children were called by the name of their eldest child, a sign of honor and fulfillment. It was significant that to the white man Kuac became Pastor Moses, but to the villagers, who at best could only say "Pathtor Motheth," he remained Kuac.

As an ordained pastor Kuac became a member of the newly formed Presbytery, to which he was responsible. The Presbytery was an organization of pastors and laymen which met to discuss the business of the church twice a year. The original Presbytery had three national pastors from two tribes, which later grew to five men from four tribes, and was supplemented by the ordained missionaries, plus laymen called "elders," who were chosen by each congregation. In the Presbyterian system the pastor's function is to teach; the elder's is to rule in all church-related matters. The absence of a common language, and the distances which removed the men one from the other presented problems that were resolved through foreign media and foreign money. English was used and translated into the dialects; transportation was provided by lorries or plane.

According to the Presbyterian system, a man must be issued a "call" to become the pastor of a congregation. For Kuac to become the official pastor at the mission church at Nasir necessitated that he receive a call from the congregation. But the people did not know what a congregation was. The idea was foreign to them. What business they did with God as a group was always done as a family or as members of the same clan. People from different clans could not think of themselves as a unit. But to facilitate matters, the Presbytery declared the group at Nasir a congregation and sent a white man to come and explain to the people how they must now call Kuac to be their pastor.

The first part of the meeting was the regular church service in the thatched-roof church. School girls in their green uniforms and bare feet wiggled and snickered in front of the simple wooden pulpit, on the mahogany four-by-fours, waiting for the service to start. Behind them, separated by a sandy aisle, was the back section of four-by-fours filled with men—teachers, clinic dressers, one or two government employees, and mission day-laborers. They were dressed in all types of clothing from one-piece outfits of limp khaki shorts, or approximations, to long trousers, white drill shorts, and long-sleeved shirts, clean, starched, and neatly pressed.

Around the limed, oval brick wall people sat on a cement bench, which was interrupted on both sides of the building by two semi-screened double doors painted green. The men sat to the right side of the pulpit, the women to the left, dividing the room in two. There were also people on the floor. Colorless in their grimy cloths, the majority of those people were to be recognized as villagers, most certainly in-patients or relatives of in-patients from the clinic. Backs straight, shoulders hunched slightly forward, they sat with expressionless faces, their hands in their laps, neither moving nor making a sound.

On the small cement platform at one end of the oval, behind the pulpit, sat Kuac in his long, white clerical robe, which was a sign of great wealth because it contained more cloth in its many folds than any villager had ever worn at one time, and beside him was the missionary, a "traveler," as Kuac later translated to the people in his introduction, in as close an approximation to "commissioner from Presbytery" as the language afforded easily. The missionary had come in by plane the day before and would leave again the next day. It was the rainy season, making travel by land impossible, and to have traveled by river would have been unreliable and time-consuming; in fact, the man might well not have been able to come at all.

Kuac took out his watch, looked at it, then tucked it back in his pocket again. Outside, the clanging of metal on an I-beam hanging on a limb of the banyan tree announced that the service was to begin. There was the sound of grinding sand on cement under leather soles as Kuac stood up and stepped behind the brown pulpit with the painted white cross in the front.

"Let us sing a song," he said, announcing a number, his voice confident, and showing a familiarity with the proceedings. He waited while the few people with the green paperbacked song-books opened to the place he had announced. Then he sang out with a strong, sure voice and the audience joined in: "It Is Always Sweet, Name of Jesus, Big Chief."

While the people sang, a baby, who had been asleep in an old woman's arms where she sat on the cement bench, wakened and began to cry. Its mother, a young woman in a faded-red cotton dress and white plastic sandals, sitting beside the older woman, took the child into her own arms and nestled it there. With a deft maneuver of her right hand she bared her breast and snuggled it into the mouth of the wailing child, watching intently in anticipation of the certain satisfying effect. On either side of her along the bench, and from the floor, other women turned their heads or looked up with sober faces, all in readiness to give advice to the young mother. But the breast muffled the child's frustrated cries, the women relaxed, and by the time the song was finished, the baby was asleep again.

Following the song Kuac said, "We shall bow our heads down. We shall pray." Sweeping his eyes across the room as he bowed his head he began, "God. Father. We have come to you now. . ."

There was an appropriate silence observed by the people and violated only at one point by three indiscreet children, joined in a skirmish over a songbook, who were brought to order by the insistent snapping of the school matron's fingers. At the end of his own prayer Kuac then began saying the Lord's Prayer, joined by some of the audience at the point, "thy kingdom come," who followed along until the sentence, "give us this day our daily bread," where a doubtful translation rendered a vague meaning and caused some to drop out. The undulation of the voices caused by the uncertainty of the worshipers created a confusion among the people on the floor, who kept looking sideways to see if it was time to lift their heads. As some had already fallen asleep during the prayer, a concerted effort was made by those sitting near them to awaken them by snapping their fingers when the prayer was over.

People waiting at the open doors then came in. One tall young man in dark glasses, wearing immaculate white shorts and shirt, brown knee stockings and black leather shoes, stood a moment in the doorway with an ebony walking stick in his hand. Before entering, he looked to see where he might sit down. Ignoring an empty section in the very back of the room, he chose a section of the four-by-fours, the third row, then headed for it, stepping cautiously around the people on the floor. When he got there, he waited momentarily for the men already seated to make room for him, necessitating one boy's getting to the floor. Then laying his stick down, he took in his fingers the back of each leg of his shorts at the crease, and folding them over so as not to ruin the crease, he sat down.

From behind the pulpit, Kuac approached the taking of the offering by saying, "We shall give our gifts to God." He called two men sitting near him on the wall bench to come and take the hemp offering baskets with the long wooden handles, which he had just taken down from the top of the wall under the thatch. Taking the baskets, the men made their way among the people sitting on the floor, reaching the baskets over their heads to more likely contributors: those in foreign clothes and the missionaries. Here and there a hand reached out and dropped something in while the rest sat stone still. After passing the baskets around, responding to a finger snap or to the loud whisper of someone who was being passed by, the men made their way back again and put the baskets on the pulpit. Kuac then prayed and the men sat down in their places.

Now the white man stood together with Kuac, who introduced him by saying that their hearts were happy because the traveler had come, and that he would speak now.

The visitor, in white shorts and shirt, black leather shoes and short black socks, stood, thick-chested, thick-calved, and meaty-armed, beside Kuac. He began by telling the people how glad he was to be there. He said this was a big day for the Christians at

Nasir and, perhaps, for the Nuer people. He remembered, he said, the time when there were only a very few Christians at Nasir. But God had worked, he said, and that was why they were there in the church that day. For this, they must be very grateful to God.

The people watched the visitor. But as time went on their attention was diverted more easily. Milk women, carrying their long-necked milk gourds on their heads, stopped in the doorway, curiously eyeing the missionary. A man in conversation with an unseen companion, walked past the window and as he did, turned his head to look in. "If he does not bring my cow," his voice drifted into the room, "I will take him before the chief."

The missionary was saying he wanted Kuac to read from two places in the Bible. Kuac then said that he would read from the "talk of God," and began reading from St. John's Gospel the seventeenth chapter. "'I do not pray for these only, but also for those who are to believe in me through their word; even as thou, Father, art in me and I in thee, that they also may be in us, so that the world may believe that thou hast sent me . . . that they may be one even as we are one.'"

The woman with the baby stood up as Kuac was reading, shifted the baby to her hip, and began moving toward the door. The women on the floor moved their legs as she came along, to give her room to walk by. Restless eyes from the audience watched her progress as she waited and stepped, waited and stepped, with her arm holding the baby whose little head lay sleepily against its mother's shoulder. "Are you going?" someone said to her.

"*Uh*," she replied.

Kuac was reading the second portion, from the Acts of the Apostles, the second chapter, about the early believers meeting faithfully together in fellowship and in prayer.

When he had finished, the missionary began to tell how the Church had come into being. The word *church* posed a problem for the translator. A church building was called "house of God." But the institution of the Church was untranslatable. "The meeting of the people of God," was the best rendition Kuac could give.

The Holy Spirit, the missionary said, had been working since Jesus' time, causing people throughout the world to believe in Jesus. Those people, wherever they were, would come together and worship. And that is the way it is today, and the Church of Jesus Christ is very big. It is not only in the Sudan, but in many places in Africa and in America and in the whole world. We are all one family, he said, and we must think about this and pray for each other and help each other as Jesus said we should do.

Then he said he had come to Nasir for an important reason. Christians, he said, when they meet, need a leader. Kuac had been chosen by God to be a pastor. Now, he said, if you Christians here at Nasir want Moses Kuac for your leader it is your responsibility to say so. If you say so before each other and before the Presbytery, it means you are asking him to come and stay and teach you. But he cannot do this unless you help him—unless he has a house to live in and money each month so that he can buy food and other things he needs for himself and his family.

The Presbytery has sent me to ask you if you agree to having Kuac be your pastor and if you will agree to give him money each month. Christians, he said, grow stronger when they give back to God some of the things He has given them. If you do not have money, he said, give eggs or pumpkins or grain, and God will be pleased.

At the end of the service, after the benediction when the white man lifted his hand over the people, a few of the well-dressed young men and one or two women came up to the front. Those who could said to the visitor, "How are you? Are you well?" And the rest said, *"Mal mi goaa?"*—Is it good peace? He smiled and answered them and they all shook his hand.

Later that same afternoon, after siesta time, another meeting was held in the church. This time only a fraction of the morning group was present, mostly baptized Christians. They were given an opportunity to ask questions. One man said, "Why is Kuac going away? Is this not his country?" The word *country* was limited in meaning to where a person was born and reared.

There was renewed effort to explain the system whereby a congregation must "call" a man to be its pastor, and if not, he will go
somewhere else. Then someone said, as in answer to the question,
"Kuac is our person, fellows, there is no argument. We want him,
is it not so?"

A man answered, *"Uh,"* and there was silence. No one knew
exactly what to say about the money either. It would hardly have
occurred to the people to pay a man just for talking about God.
They paid to get God to work. Men who spoke the "talk of God," the
prophets, the holy men of the people, were engaged by a family to
perform a specific sacrifice or special rite on their behalf, and were
paid in money and/or cattle and cloth and spears. The people then
expected to be shown the power of God in a supernatural way, or
by a message from Him which would bring an end to their difficulty.
In that as Christians they were now to believe that God works by
the faith of His people, it would seem likely that they would wonder
at having to pay a pastor at all.

But the subject was discussed and the missionary proposed a
plan as from the Presbytery, that the congregation was to pay one
half of the pastor's salary each month, and the Presbytery would
pay the other half. The amount each would pay was six pounds, or
approximately eighteen dollars. Some of the people expressed an
ignorance as to where the money would come from, but the exhor-
tation was given to them that they must learn to give, and that in
giving they would know God's blessing.

In an unprecedented act of generosity a year or so later, a man
brought a cow to church one Sunday and said he was giving it as a
gift to God. It was a white cow with a calf at its side, which bawled
intermittently throughout the service. In communal agreement
Reet, the elder, took the cow and its calf to his village where he
tethered it with his small herd. One morning shortly thereafter,
early, as the red ball of the sun peeked over the rim of the earth,
Reet awakened and went out to the cattle tethered in front of his
barn. They lay where they had slept, their front legs bent under

them in the soft ashes they themselves had ground to powder with their cloven hoofs. But the white cow and its calf were gone. In the ashes were the large, bare footprints of a man, which the giver of the cow readily recognized as those of one of his relatives. In a vain search across the country he inquired about the animals, but no one had seen them. They had vanished into thin air.

Predictably, the people were unmoved at this. Even the giver shrugged his shoulders at my annoyance. They all knew a man could not choose to give a cow away without the family's consent. And to give a cow to God? How can you give a cow to God unless you kill it? Besides, when it is killed the people get to eat it, but to give a cow to the white man's God was like losing it for nothing—so in the night the family came and took it back.

However, in the meeting on that Sunday afternoon, faced with the alternative (senseless, to them) of losing Kuac altogether, the people unanimously agreed that they wanted him to stay, and that they would pay half his salary of thirty-six dollars a month.

Then the white members of Presbytery made up a set of rules whereby the people were to live and to experience the reigning of Jesus Christ in their lives. The idea of Jesus Christ reigning as king in one's life is a good one; it comes from the Scripture, but the question is, How does this come to pass? Does it happen by obeying a certain arbitrary set of rules? How does a person *decide* that he's not going to be afraid of death?

When Kuac received the rules, he translated them and read them to the people.

To let Jesus Christ reign as King in our lives and Savior of our souls we shall daily live in the following manner by the help of the Holy Spirit:

We shall trust Jesus and obey Him in all He commands of us, thinking primarily of the two Great Commandments and then all the other commands of our Lord. [Mark 12:29–31; 1 John 5:3.] We want to increase our knowledge of God our Father and His Son and therefore we will plan our work so that with our families we will be present at all church meetings and village prayer meetings. [Colossians 1:9–10; Hebrews 10–25.] In our separate homes we will have daily family prayers at sunup. We will read God's Word and praise Him for our salvation in Christ, ask for forgiveness of our sins and the power and guidance of the Holy Spirit for the work of the day. At meal times, whenever we eat, we will stop to thank our Lord for the provision of our needs from His hand and ask His blessing on the food and those who have prepared it. [Mark 1:35.]

At the birth of a child the elders of the church and nearby Christians will join together with the parents thanking and praising God for the new little life He has given them to raise for Him. When the mother and child are strong the child will be baptized in the Church. [Acts 16:15; 2:39.]

As parents we will teach our children the truth about Jesus who loves them and died for them. [Acts 2:38–39.] When the children are old enough to marry we will encourage and help them to marry one who also loves Jesus so that the new family will be strong in Jesus and not divided and weak. The Church teaches that marriage with full consent by both the young woman's and man's parents has the Church's blessing. The introductory advances are made openly and honestly before the Church and our Lord, seeking both's blessing. [1 Thessalonians 4:1–6; Mark 3:25.]

God requires us to give Him one-tenth of all we grow in our fields and one-tenth of all money we earn. If we do as He says He will bless the remainder. [Malachi 3:6–10.] In our daily work we will work as if for Jesus in whatever work He has called us to do. As young men we will ask God's guidance as to what kind of work we should do.

We will take a firm stand against drunkenness and over-indulgence of any kind. [Romans 6:12–14; 13:11–14; Ephesians 4:25–32.] We will witness for Jesus by word and action in our villages, to visitors and friends and wherever we are. We will tell of our King, our Savior Jesus Christ, and all He has done for us. In the dry season particularly, we will join together to plant God's Word in places where people do not know it. [Acts 1:8.] We will look forward to and pray for the return of Jesus that He may come soon. When death comes to a loved one we will not be afraid but be thankful and happy for the one who has gone before us to be with God in His Home. We each one look for the day when we also will be in the Place Jesus has prepared for us in His Father's Home. [John 14; Hebrews 13:20–21.]

10

IN THE BEGINNING

The Nuer had their own legends of the creation story. In them, if God is mentioned, He is always benevolent, kind, and sometimes naive. The stories are fantasies, revealing the delightful imagination of a people whose real life is eminently hard.

Not everyone knew these stories. One day I asked Man Gaac if she could tell me how the world began. I wanted to record it on tape. But when she sat down and tried to tell me, she could not do it. She remonstrated with me, saying I had taken her "unawares, as a lion does its prey"; had I forewarned her, she said, she would have inquired from others, as one does who desires answers to what the talk of God means and seeks out a friend to help him. I told her I understood, that she could go and come again when she was ready.

When she came again she told me the following story, this time with no hesitation:

"The people came out from somewhere at the heglig tree of Liiy. When they came out, they came out as trees. They came out with their cattle together, and they had no stomachs.

"Stomachs lived in the wilderness. They pastured on grass. There was no fire, and all foods prepared themselves. There was no person to eat them.

"One day a woman departed and went to the plain, and brought back a stomach. 'Come, my sister,' she said, 'eat my portion of food which no one is able to eat.' She gave the stomach everything. She gave it the porridge. She filled it up with butter oil, and stomach ate it.

"At nightfall the woman told stomach, 'Return to your place.'

"Stomach said, 'I will not.'

"Stomach refused to go back to the plain.

"Night came and the people went to sleep. Then stomach returned to the plain and told the other stomachs that the people were asleep. They then came to where the people were sleeping and each stomach went into a person.

"In the morning the people awoke after having dreamed great dreams. They did not know that it was the food which had made them sleep so well.

"After that people ate their food.

"There was no fire. The people melted their food by the heat of the sun, then cooked it with milk under the sun and ate it. When things were this way it happened that a dog was caught in the rain. It ran and squeezed itself into a red cobra's house. When it was in the cobra's house, the cobra came and put sticks on the fire. Then the dog fanned the fire with his tail, and stuck his tail into the flames to catch his tail on fire.

"When it came outside, it began setting fire to the forest, and the fire burned in the forest. When the people saw it, each one said he must go and get himself some fire. After that pots were set to cook on the fire and the food was cooked in them.

"Work worked itself. It was not done by people. One day a young woman who had just been married came into the family. She said, 'I will carry my mother-in-law's things on my head. The things of my mother-in-law will not have to walk by themselves any more as they used to.'

"She picked up her mother-in-law's cook pots and gourds and put them on her head. But they all jumped down again. So she gathered them all together and picked them up again and put them on her head. They jumped down again, and again she picked them up. Finally they got tired of this, and the things of the other people got tired of it too. Then they all said, 'Oh, who will ever walk again?' No one needs to walk any more. Let us all be carried from now on.'

"When the people arrived at the village, the woman took her spear and went out to cut some roofing grass. When she had cut the grass she came back and marked out the circle for her hut; then she dug it around. After she had dug it, she stood up the sticks for the wall. Then she put on the frame for the roof.

"The other people were waiting for their houses to build themselves. The woman was the only one in a hut. The others were outside being killed for nothing by the sun, even though it never used to hurt them. When they saw what the woman had done, the next morning they took their spears and went out to cut grass. Then they made their own huts.

"The people always walked softly. They just touched the earth with their feet lest they pierce it through. It happened that when the people made their first village, the cow of the young married woman got into some kind of trouble. The people called her, 'Young woman! Young woman! Young woman! Your cow is in trouble! Your cow is in trouble!'

"The woman ran with a great running to get the cow. The people cried out, 'Young woman, you will pierce the earth! You will pierce the earth!' But when they saw that she did not pierce the earth, they too began to run and walk heavily upon it."

Another creation legend I heard from an old man who came to my house one day not a little pleased that he had been sought out to recall the tales of antiquity. There was nothing between him and the ancients, for he was as one of them, never having been educated and never having seen the outside world.

He said, "When God was creating everybody, He created the things with hair. He created the birds and the animals and they had hair. When He conceived us, the Nuer and the foreigner, we were conceived as twins. But we were smooth.

"God said to the dog, 'Dog.'

"The dog said, 'Uh?'

"These twins, I made them premature. Take them and hang them up. I caused these premature ones to be smooth. Everything else I bore with hair.

"The dog went and hung up the twins in the crotch of a wild thorn tree. He carried milk to them in a milk gourd. They drank the milk every day, every day until they had grown into children. When they had grown into children, God said, 'So, now I will go and see the place where the dog takes the milk.'

"The dog went with the milk along the side of the path and took it to the children. They drank it all and then they began to play. When they began to play, then God jumped in with them. He went to slap the dog, and the dog wagged his tail against the ground, pleading with God.

"Then God said, 'So be it, take them to the village and let them be a part of the village.'

"So he took them to the village.

"The fox said to his children, 'My children, let your children's children sharpen sticks for themselves. We will taste the ones who have hair, and we will leave the bitter ones. So they found that the lion was bitter, the hyena was bitter, the leopard was bitter, the fox was bitter. Then they said, 'Let us leave this.'

"God said to the cape buffalo, 'My child, Two-feet will kill you.' He referred to mankind. 'You come here. Take these spears.'

"The buffalo said, 'All right, but I will get them later.'

"Night fell. The fox departed and went to man's house and said, 'You.'

"'*Uh*,' man said.

"The fox said, 'Spears are being given to the buffalo.'

"Man departed and went to God.

"'Father.'

"'*Uh*,' God said.

"'Give me the spears.'

"'Who are you?'

"'I am buffalo.'

"'Oh, you are buffalo?'

"'*Uh*.'

"'*Uh*, here take these spears.'

Man took the spears.

"The buffalo came late at night and God said, 'It is you?'

"And buffalo said, '*Uh*.'

"'Who are you?' God said.

"'I am buffalo.'

"'But who was the person of before. Was it not you?'

"'No, it was not I.'

"'Oh, it was not you. Well, since it was not you, I will give you these horns.' He put the horns on the buffalo's head. 'You will aid yourself with these.' He turned the horns outward.

"But the fox said, 'No. You won't gore men. If you and they get into an argument, you won't gore them. Let your horns be turned inward.' So he turned his horns inward."

"How things were divided: Man was given water and fire. The lion was given a cow. The hyena was given a goat. The weaverbird was given the dura grain. Then they all became thirsty.

"When they became thirsty, the lion came to man and said, 'Let me have a drink.'

" 'No, you can't drink.'

" 'Let me buy it.'

" 'No, you can't buy it.'

" 'You. Take the cow. I will drink.'

"Man agreed and took the cow. Then the hyena came.

" 'Man.'

" '*Uh.*'

" 'Let me drink.'

" 'No, there is no water.'

" 'Oh, there is no water?'

" '*Uh*, there is no water.'

" 'Oh, take the goats, I will hunt them from you.'

"The weaverbird came.

" 'Man. Let me drink.'

" 'No, you can't drink.'

" 'Oh, take my dura grain. I will hunt it from you. I will drink.' "

The old man took a long time in telling his stories. He was pleased with them and would repeat some of the phrases a second time, then pause to chuckle as if the state of affairs today between man and the animals—that the lion eats man's cattle, the hyena eats man's goats, and the weaverbird eats man's dura grain—makes the story credible.

They must have been great people, those first animals! I wondered, did the man attacked by the buffalo and tossed into the air, find comfort in the fact that the horns now tossing him were turned inward by order of the fox, and thus less dangerous?

At the end of our session together I gave the old man a bed sheet, the brightness and length of which so pleased him that he laughed aloud. He draped it around himself, tying it with a large knot at his chest, and left the house with his walking stick, a patriarch in his own right.

Kuac and I translated the book of Genesis. It did not present the linguistic problems or the complicated metaphysics one finds in the New Testament. It told the kind of story the people more readily understood, the story of men and women, of cattle, spirits, and God; and it was basic to one's understanding of the New Testament.

Kuac taught the creation story to the people, but contrary to what one might like to think, it was not something they could receive as their own. It was a foreign story; more of the talk of the white man's God. They accepted it as this in all good faith, saying it was "good talk," but coming from the mouth of Kuac to their ears was not sufficient reason to cause them to believe that they were hearing a revelation from God. After all, the Dinka people had their story. The Anuak had theirs. The Shilluk had theirs. So it was understandable that the white man would have his story too. It was not an argument as to whose story was the right one; they all were. They did chuckle knowingly over the role the snake played in bringing about Eve's downfall, because the snake came to Eve as the Nuer believe their snakes come to them, as a god not a creature, bringing death and God's wrath. This supported the fear they already had of snakes. They would refer to any particular snake as "father-of-badness," the name we used for the devil in our translation.

We also translated hopefully the book of Exodus where God shows to men their need to be holy before Him, and the consequent necessity of blood sacrifice on a holy altar. But the problem of communication persisted, of getting the people to realize that this message was for them.

Of the few who recognized the Bible to be the Word of God, and who wanted the Scriptures translated into their own language, Kuac was the one who persevered with me in trying to ensure that the translation was accurate and structurally sound. It must read as though a Nuer had said it, we agreed.

We discussed such words as *grace* and *hope*, trying to find a way to say them.

"Grace, Nyarial," Kuac would say, "is like the *wuot Kuoth.*"

"You mean the manliness of God?" I asked.

"Yes, maybe."

And I would think, What does manliness mean to a Nuer person? Not a physique, but the totality of virtue and strength. Could this possibly be grace? Would it make any sense to say, The manliness of God saved us? And if not, what would make sense?

We could not decide. It was not that we had an extensive vocabulary to choose from. We had to approximate meanings as best we could.

For example, I tried for some time to find a way to say "conscience." The Nuer use one word, *heart*, to express feelings. They say, "My heart burned," to express anger. "My heart fell," to express joy. "My heart is bad," to express displeasure. They had no description for conscience or the working of conscience. I tried to make one up by using a verb commonly identified with an irritating habit the people had of pecking incessantly on someone's arm or shoulder with the forefinger to attract his attention. I asked Man Gaac, "Would it not occur, if you took some money off my desk which was not yours, that when you thought upon it later something would peck at your heart?"

"Yes," she said without hesitation. And without hesitation I relaxed in a moment of unguarded ecstasy, thinking that at last I had found the answer. However, on second thought I checked with her again.

"What would your heart be saying to you?" I said.

"It would say, 'Go back and get some more,' " she answered.

There were other problems, too. For example, it was not possible to say, "the father." It was always necessary to say whose father. Thus in John's Gospel, "Show us the Father" had to be rendered, "Show us our Father." (The capital letter was irrelevant to the meaning as far as the people understood.)

It was impossible to translate the word *disciple*, meaning learner. The culture had no place for an adult learner. As Man Gaac explained to me, an adult who advises another adult on how to do something is met by the retort: "Do you excel me? Were you born [conceived] with this work?" It is an insult to suppose that you can teach an adult, the idea being that when one reaches adulthood he should have all the necessary skills pertinent to existence. Prophets did have followers who walked from place to place together, but their main objective, Man Gaac said, was having a source of food. The prophet [*gök*] fed them. Another type of followers was called "sent ones." They were the prophet's lords-in-waiting. One day I watched a prophet walking through a village with a retinue of these men. And later I sat in the hut where he was and watched him give an order. I had come to visit the prophet and to ask him questions, and at the end of our conversation, in which he admitted to being God and to having created us all, he gave a command to one of the young men, who obeyed, went out, and came back later with a handful of tobacco, which the prophet sprinkled on my head in blessing, and with a twenty-piaster piece, which the prophet gave to me as a gift.

Translation problems were not only confined to words per se, but included syntax. The Nuer speak in short sentences. They use the passive voice where, in English, the active voice would be used. The predicate was emphasized by using the passive voice, but the subject was emphasized by using the active voice. "It was eaten," you would say if you wanted to explain what had happened to the food. But if the emphasis was on the fact that a certain person ate it, you would say, "He ate it."

Also the verbs recorded a kind of action, not the time of action, as in English. "Where are you staying, last year?" you would say. "I am staying here," would be the answer.

Another example of how, in translation, one must be prepared to adapt one language to another is found in St. Peter's letters. The Nuer version could not begin with an abrupt salutation as the Greek does. The Nuer have no history of letter writing and hence no formal device for writing conversation, so the translator must put down on paper exactly what people say to each other in greeting. So the letter begins, "It is I, Peter. I am writing you a paper."

Perhaps one of the more frustrating aspects of translation was the weakness of certain key words. Meanings of words develop from people's experience. It was not surprising that the Nuer word for "love" was lacking in meaning. The word meant not only to love, but to agree to. I learned of the weakness of this word while I was still very new in Africa.

One afternoon I heard a pitiful wail coming from a clinic hut. My speaking ability was limited, but I went out to see what was the matter. Inside the hut, sitting alone on the bare floor, was a woman holding a little girl against her naked breast. The girl was dead. Tears coursed the mother's cheeks and dropped onto the body of the child, making shiny, black lines across her skin. The woman sobbed and cried out through her tears, *"Ayow! Ayow! Ayow!* She died. My child died. *Ayow! Ayowl"* And she lifted a palm in supplication.

Obviously she loved the little girl, and because she loved her, her heart was broken. "This one is my only daughter," she cried. "It is she, my daughter. *Ay. Ay."*

I said to her the only thing I knew to say: "Old mother, God loves you." But as soon as I said it, I knew that the word *love* was being challenged. It was on trial in her life. She suffered because she loved. She suffered because God did not love, she thought. He had taken her child. He had taken all of her children. He takes children of every woman, in every generation. He sends life only to follow it hard with death.

How does one exist in this atmosphere? How does one dare to love? He cannot. It is too devastating. The heart cannot survive being broken. It is best not to love. So love was suppressed and ways were devised to fortify oneself and others against death. For example, drawing attention to babies and little children was strictly avoided. You did not admit that a baby was fat. You never counted the number of children gathered in one place. You did everything to divert God's attention away from them, not to them. Children were given ominous names like: You Will Die; You Will Not Live; Death; Grave; Tears; Weeping. No one was called Happiness or Peace or You Will Live.

People did not do things for love. They did not marry for love. So although it was possible to translate "God is love," the message of the verse was dubious.

The many problems of translation exploded my theories of Bible translating, and precluded the possibility of producing an exact and therefore inerrant—as Evangelicals used the term—translation of the Scriptures.

11

MARRIED TO A DEAD MAN

It was an effort for me to assimilate a concept as foreign as polygamy. It was more of an effort to assimilate all of its ramifications. At home in America, polygamy had been easily defined and readily condemned, and I was early prejudiced against it. It was an evil practice, of the devil. If you did not concur with this definition, you certainly were not a spiritual Christian.

The African pastor inherited the problem of polygamy from the missionaries—he was unaware of it as a problem until the missionaries came—and another, more vital problem, as well; one which did not concern the missionaries because it did not clash with doctrine. It was the problem of the single woman, inherent in the monogamous system. If women were not to be wives and mothers, what alternative reason for being was a pastor to suggest to them in a land where there were no careers to offer as possible solutions, if, indeed, careers are a solution?

If polygamy was evil, was not monogamy more so?

Kuac would discuss the knotty problems our Christian monogamous rules created at the mission, explaining the custom of the people to us, but he never became alarmed and never made any judgments. He never spoke of polygamy as sin, and he never preached about it. In fact, polygamy had never truly become a part of his thinking. Polygamy was the white man's word and did not accurately describe the complex system of marriage with which Kuac was familiar.

One day I asked him about a certain woman who had been coming to my Bible class. She told me that she wanted to be baptized, but in the course of telling me this she also said that her husband was leaving her, literally abandoning her. I asked, "Is he divorcing you?" And she replied No, that he was just leaving her.

A man would never leave his wife without getting his cattle back. I did not understand what this woman, whose name was Nyadak, meant and so I asked Kuac about it.

"Why is he leaving her?" I wanted to know.

Kuac sat relaxed on his chair, feet crossed on the floor, his hands in his lap. "Because he is going to marry," he said, as if I understood.

"But it does not go into my heart at all," I said. "I thought she *was* his wife. If he marries another wife he won't leave the one he already has, will he?"

"No, but Nyadak is not his wife. Nyadak's family married her to a man who was already dead. He had 'nothinged.' So in order to raise up children to the man, his own brother took Nyadak for him. Do you not see it?"

"You say, 'Do I not see it?' I've never heard of such a thing before. She was married to a dead man?"

"*Uh*, that man died before he had ever married, and after his death he was married. Now that man's brother wants to marry a wife for himself. He does not want his brother's wife any more. Now he will go and live with his own wife and leave Nyadak." He paused at the end of his story, then added, "Does it not go into your heart well?"

I laughed. "I suppose it goes into my heart, but it is amazing talk. Was she married with cattle even though the man was dead?"

"*Uh*, she was married with cattle."

"And there was a dance?"

"*Uh*," he said with a slight upward nod of his head.

What a different orientation to life, I thought. I could never be a part of it. It is not enough just to have children, I would want a companion. But this way is legitimate for her; she is satisfied.

"How many children does Nyadak have?" I said.

"I think she has three children, but one child is blind."

"What happened to it?"

"Nothing. I think it just became blind for no reason."

"That is hard to do," I said. "I think it was the flies."

"*Uh,* maybe it was," he laughed.

The word *flies* diverted the conversation into a request for DDT powder. The bedbugs in his house had become unbearable, Kuac said. They were in the walls and the thatch, and they would not come out. The solution the health officers used was too weak. Kuac wanted some of mine. I promised him some if he had ten piasters. Then we returned to Nyadak's problem, about which, between the two of us, I was the more greatly concerned.

"What will Nyadak do? Can she not be married again?" I queried. But even as I asked the question, I realized the answer: she would have to be divorced.

"A divorce would not be easy for her," Kuac said. "I think her brothers would not agree. They would have to find the cattle of the marriage and return them. This would be hard. It means they would have to take the cattle from their own marriages which would make much trouble. "No," he said, looking out the window, "they would not agree to it. Anyway, she would not be married again for much cattle. If she were still a girl, then there would be no problem; but she is old." He slid his feet under the table and leaned back in his chair. "*Ah,* my back is sore," he said. "Let me get a drink."

He got up and went out to the veranda where the clay pot of water was. A gust of hot air blew into the room through the big screen window. "It is good water," Kuac said, coming back into the room and sitting down in his chair. "The water of the river and the water of the well, they are not the same. I like the water of the river."

"Is the water pot not empty?" I said. "I did not bring any water today."

"It wants to be empty, but there is still some in it," he said. Another hot blast came into the room, and the dry seedpods on the tree at the back of the house rattled through the far screen window.

"So what happens to Nyadak?" I went on. "She must be worrying about not having more children, isn't she?"

"Maybe that is so, but her body is still strong; she will find children," he said. He sat up in his chair again. "Oh," he said, looking out the window.

"What now?" I said, trying to see around the corner of the window, but my view was blocked by the side of the veranda.

"That woman! That woman!" He called loudly. Then to me he said, "There is a woman walking with grass. I need it for my house." Watching from his chair he called to her again. "Bring it here. Bring it here." The corners of his mouth held in a smile. Obviously the woman on the path did not know where the voice was coming from, and Kuac was enjoying her confusion. "Here I am," he called again. "Come to this house."

"She is coming," he said to me, watching every move she made with a bright look on his face. "Here, by the window," he said, directing her.

I could see the woman now. She was standing outside the screen with a large bundle of thatching grass on her head. She had cut it out on the plain, tied it together with a braided grass rope, and brought it in to sell.

"Are you selling it?" Kuac asked.

"*Uh,*" she said, looking blankly into the screen.

"How much is it?"

"Three piasters," she said. Almost ten cents.

"But it is a little head," Kuac protested, not yet moving from his chair. "I will give you two piasters."

She turned slowly around and began walking away. She would have none of his bargaining. Kuac called after her. "You, that woman. Come back. I will buy it." Then turning to me he said, "Nyarial, give me three piasters."

"I think there are three piasters in that little can on the table there. Look and see." He fished out three copper coins.

"Good," he said to himself, then he said to me in English, "Excuse me, Nyarial, I will come again quickly." He hurried away. I took out my record book and jotted down: Kuac, the date, three

piasters—grass. There was a thud. I looked up. The old woman
had dropped the head of grass to the ground. She stood, holding
her chin with the first three fingers of her right hand. I looked
at her and thought, Old woman, you are wondering and so am
I. I am wondering about you. What is your idea of marriage? I
think I know. You want to have children. You would say to me:
"Why aren't you married? Do you not like children? Are children
not good?"

I understand you. Yes, children are good. They are proof of a
woman's fulfillment. They make you a woman. You, old woman,
your breasts are flabby. You have nursed many children. Kuac called
you "Woman." You are a success. You are secure. A man's name will
be carried forward to the next generation because of you. In this
you are satisfied.

She put out her hand and received the coins from Kuac. Nothing was said between them. Then she spread them out in her palm,
looked at them to see if they were right, and closed her fist. She
untied the knot at her chest in the corner of the cloth she wore,
wrapped the coins in it, and tied it up again.

"Take it to my house," Kuac said.

"It is so," she said, then stooped, picked up the grass-carrying
ring and put it on her head. Bending down she took hold of the
grass bundle with both hands—it stood upright on the ground—
and placed her head firmly at the thick, butt end. Then with a
mighty effort she lifted her back, her head, the bundle into the air
and walked away with great dignity.

The screen door banged and Kuac again came into the room.

"It is good," he said. "The roof of my house is bad—that is why
I wanted that grass. It is much trouble. I am sorry, Nyarial."

"It is all right," I said. I was thinking of him now as the ordained pastor of the church and what he would do about baptizing
someone like Nyadak. "What do you think, Kuac, about baptizing
Nyadak?" I asked. "She wants to believe in Jesus, but what if she
continues to follow the ways of men? Is this good?"

"But it is the way of our people," he said simply, and sat down. "Our women will not easily find the path of God," he added. "It is too hard for them. Maybe their children will."

"Why do you say that about the children?"

"Because we will teach them."

"You will teach them the words of the Bible, is that what you mean?"

"*Uh*, that is it," he said confidently, echoing the slogan of modern civilization: to change people, teach them.

This led me to say, "Kuac, if you have a daughter, will you agree to her being married to a dead man, as Nyadak was?"

"But it is not just my talk, Nyarial," he said. "It is the talk of the whole family. I might refuse if the talk of the cattle is not good. But it is big talk, not just the talk of one person."

"That is true," I agreed. "And about Nyadak, what will you do?"

"I think she will be baptized. Reet agrees to this," he said, speaking of the church elder, a man respected by the villagers as a true believer. "She is related to him. Her husband was his uncle, his mother's brother. She first went to Reet. She sat by him and he talked with her about God. She is not afraid. She says she will not go to the sacrifices of her people. She has left those gods."

I turned this over in my mind. She has come to Jesus like the blind man, like the woman who touched the hem of His garment. He will not turn her away. Then I thought again of Reet, the church elder.

"Could it be," I said, "that Reet might now be the one to father her children for her husband, his uncle?" My mind wrestled with the idea.

But Kuac answered me nonchalantly, "It could be like that," he said.

12

A MOTHER IN TWO WORLDS

Man Gaac, who took me to the initiation, is a woman who laughed with me, who talked with me, who cared devoutly for her five children, and who clasped the hand of her only granddaughter as she clasped none other. She was tall and big and carried much weight, for, unlike her contemporaries who sat by day nursing their children's children and smoking their wooden pipes, and for whom less food was required, Man Gaac, in the most recent years, had been the original matron of the first girls' boarding school at Nasir, for which she received a salary, and because of which she had eaten regularly and well.

She was a Dinka by birth. But at an early age she and her sister had come into the Nuer tribe by way of tribal warfare, when, before foreign government imposed a greater control, the Nuers raided the Dinkas, killing their men and gaining for themselves their cattle, their women and children.

Her marriage took place in Nuer country, at the hands of the relatives of the man who had captured her. It was a marriage which brought dissension in the family, for her captor was not in agreement with the man to whom she was married. Upon her a shadow was cast, which had not yet lifted even this late in her life, a shadow in the form of blame for being the cause of a family war. The war had occurred, it was claimed, because of jealousy between Man Gaac and another wife who was childless. The woman left the family and went away. Her husband went after his cattle from the marriage, but he was refused. Then followed the war.

"They call it 'my war,'" Man Gaac told me, "that I brought it; but there is nothing which I spoiled, which I can find in my head, which I can think of. There is nothing which I spoiled that I know.

"Certainly," she continued, "if you caused there to be adultery, is it not your sin? Or if you stole and the war came of it, is it not on your head? But there is not one thing in which I sinned.

"*They* said it with their mouths, they and their family, 'It is your war.'

"I asked them, 'It is my war how? I, what did I do? Tell me what I did. Is there something I stole? Did I act in adultery which brought the talk between the man and his wife?' A girl divorces herself, and the man goes and asks for his cattle, how can that be anything of mine? Is it my doing because the cattle were divorced behind my back? Is that the meaning? Is that why this talk against me goes on and on?"

I asked her, "Is the talk still, does it persist?"

"They say it up to this day, 'Absolutely, absolutely it is your fault.'"

Man Gaac was a believer. She had five children, four sons and a daughter. Gac, her eldest son, had come to school at the mission, then worked for a time in the clinic and later went on to government school. He was the first believer in his family, a friend of Kuac's, and it was he who encouraged his mother to believe. It was at a time when her daughter's life hung in the balance. She had tetanus and was brought to the clinic upon Gac's insistence, and fed through a tube on the floor of the hut where she lay. In time she recovered and Man Gaac's faith in the white man's God took root.

She was illiterate although she worked at learning to read for years. She could "read" the first few verses of the Gospel of John reasonably well. She had her own well-thumbed copy and you would see her sitting, reading those first verses, pointing out the words with her thick forefinger. She had a bed in one corner of the girls' dormitory where she lived during the school year. Her things she kept locked in a green metal box under her wooden bed. The key to it was on a ring with other school keys tied on a string at her waist. She walked home to the village many times a week.

Man Gaac was responsible for each girl in the school. She mediated their quarrels and if they needed a higher court, led the offenders through the orchard to the headmistress. Without her presence the headmistress would not hear any complaint. What were the complaints? Usually very personal ones. So-and-so refuses to grind her share of grain for the evening meal. So-and-so hit so-and-so and made her cry. So-and-so cursed so-and-so.

Man Gaac lived among them, shouting over their shouts and wearying over their daily squabbles. She was prepared to suffer for them too. I watched her one night on her knees, inside the cook hut where a fire had started and was threatening the entire area of dormitories, pulling burning thatch out of the roof and putting it out with her hands.

Every Sunday she was at the church, sitting with the little girls on the mahogany four-by-fours in her cotton dress she had made by hand. And every Sunday, following the service, she was at the Bible class, sitting in the wicker chair by the window.

She was shrewd. One morning in class I said, "Tell your neighbors, 'Come, we are praying, let us go together.' " Man Gaac was not impressed.

"No, Nyarial," she said candidly, "they will not come. They will come only if God calls them. They say, 'It is the white man's talk, what is that to us?' "

When Man Gaac was chosen as a deaconess in the church, she did not understand what that meant. I attempted to show her. We went visiting in the village, calling on people who had come to the church. One woman was baptized but gave no indication of what this meant to her, and instead confused the issue by questionable conduct, failing as a reputable person in the eyes of her own people. She was a schemer, which everybody knew. However, when her husband died, Man Gaac and I went to see her. I purposely left my Scripture portion at home. The woman knew much of the available Scripture by heart. I said to Man Gaac, "I left the paper at home."

"It is good," she replied.

"You will talk to her," I said. "You will know what to say."

"What is the meaning of that?" Man Gaac asked. "That woman? Her heart is very hard. There is nothing she will hear. I have no talk for her."

Man Gaac had to straddle two worlds—the world of the village, and the new world of the town. At home her youngest son had yet to be initiated into the tribe; whereas her oldest son, Gac (the one who had once been employed at the mission clinic but had left), was now a policeman in Malakal, two hundred miles away. Man Gaac knew nothing about Malakal where Gac lived. She had never been there, or to any town anywhere. She could not envision the kind of life Gac was living; she was content if she could but hear how he was.

She would come to my house and dictate letters to him.

"Gac, my son," she would say, "Are you at peace? We are all at peace here. Your brother, Gatluak, came back from his journey. He 'found' a cow. He brought his wife. Why have you not written me a paper? Is it peace? The grain is not enough. You must send us money to buy grain. When are you coming back? Remain in peace. I am Man Gaac."

Gac did not answer his mother's letters. Man Gaac became worried. I went to Malakal and she sent Gac a message by me.

The Nile River flowed quietly past the little town of Malakal, carrying papyrus, sudd, and water hyacinths on its muddy surface. Each night, across the river, the red ball of the sun sank out of sight at the far edge of the empty plain. Large stern wheelers, pushing heavy barges, moved in and out of the dock on scheduled days, while swarms of southern tribesmen and northern Arabs milled about the area, deserting the streets and shops. One main road, which was hard-topped, went through the town and out, continuing in both directions as a single dirt track, the Cape-to-Cairo route through the Sudan.

In the center of the town were two large Greek shops stocked with Asian and European goods, and around them, and on parallel streets, low, flat-topped Arab shops stood snugly together. The shops divided the town. To one side of them, and along the river, were the expensive residences of the government officials. Behind the shops, away from the river and next to the barren plain, was the section where the Africans lived. Here, on a great block of land separated by clay streets, were rows of mud-and-thatch houses which were set apart one from the other by grass mats hung up as fences. Students, laborers, government employees from many tribal areas lived here, joined by transients—restless schoolboys wanting jobs, hospital patients from far away villages needing places to stay while receiving treatment.

There was a freedom and sophistication afforded those who lived here, and a questionable future.

It was early afternoon the day I walked down one of those clay streets to the house where Gac lived. I had not been there before. A transistor radio blared out Arabic music from somewhere as I clapped at the doorway in the matted fence and Gac appeared. He was tall, almost handsome, but his face was too round. He smiled a lot and whistled through his teeth, so that to remember him is to see a pleasant friendly face and to hear a laugh—a fast, giggling sound in the bass clef. We were not strangers. Through the years Gac and I had talked together and discussed many things. He had visited the revival area in Ruanda with Kuac and both of them returned sobered by what they had seen. I remember talking with Gac about his experience there. We sat on a barge of a river steamer, going up the Nile, he on his way back to government school, and I to another mission station. He was considering, in those days, the spiritual value of things, stirred by what he had seen among the Christian Africans in Ruanda. He had the happy, seeking spirit of a young man then, as yet untouched by the battering forces of life, which were to strike him later and knock him down.

"Is it peace, my sister?" he greeted me, lifting his eyebrows above his dancing eyes in a characteristic expression as he shook my hand. "You have come."

"*Uh*, it is peace, my brother," I said, crossing the few steps from the fence to his house, "and I have truly come. Are you at peace?"

"*Uh*, we are truly at peace," he said, his eyes still dancing.

Inside the house I sat down on the bed where Gac directed me. The room was small. The Arab-type bed sat in one corner. Its thin cotton mattress was covered with a red satin spread frayed at the edges, and on top of it a hard pillow, with a sewed-on cover, very brown and badly spotted. In the middle of the room was a wooden table, painted green, and on top of the table was an enamel tray, holding two grubby glasses and a teapot. Sticking out from under the tray was a paper Gospel of John. A kerosene pressure lantern hung on a wire from the ceiling, and a new bicycle stood against the back wall. The bicycle was black, had a headlamp and a bell, and a blue vinyl cover on the seat. Above the bicycle, on the wall, was a printed colored portrait of General Aboud, the then military head of the Sudan government. At the top of the picture, and in line with its side edges, was a paper Sudanese flag of horizontal blue, yellow, and green bars.

Gac sat down beside me on the bed. "How are you?" he inquired in English.

"I am well," I answered.

"When did you come?" he said.

"I came yesterday on the airplane," I said.

"Oh," he said, "I work at the airdrome."

"I did not see you there." The airdrome was very small. Usually the policemen on duty stood outside on the porch of the low bungalow-style building.

"No, the little plane was already in the hangar when I came on duty," he explained.

A young woman whom I did not know came into the house as we were talking, carrying a baby on her hip. Her hair was anchored in rows of tiny braids over her head like an Arab woman's; her machine-made dress of bright yellow rayon had no buttons, no placket, no zipper. It was trimmed with red binding, and hung like a sack over her slim body. There were metal bangles around her ankles and white, plastic sandals, unbuckled on her feet.

She put the baby down on the floor and walked away. The child turned its head to find her and, discovering her gone, puckered his face, determined to cry. Tears trickled down each cheek in no time. Presently they splashed onto his bare chest and rolled sporadically over his round, little belly to the band of his oversized khaki shorts which hung precariously around his hipless bottom.

"Pick up the child," Gac ordered.

The woman turned back sullenly to the child, picked him up and took out a breast from the low-cut yellow dress, put it to his mouth, and rubbed his teary cheeks dry with the side of her hand. Then she walked away, through the hanging curtain in the doorway of the back mud wall, carrying the quieted child heavily on her right hip.

Gac was wearing an old pair of khaki shorts and a white undershirt. On his feet were big, shiny policeman's leather sandals with the heavy cleats. The full-sized front door was opened back against the wall, and the sun came through the doorway and fell in a rectangular shape across the bed, framing us in its light. It fell on Gac, on his white undershirt and his black satiny shoulder and smooth upper arm with the square scarred design pricked onto it. It fell on his wide, flat nose, his white teeth and smooth cheek with its circle of scarred dots. It fell across his ear with the empty hole in its lobe, and across the six horizontal initiation scars on his forehead. His body was "empty" except for a gold-colored ring with a red glass stone on his finger. He wore no beads and no bracelets. His hair was combed and a red, plastic comb was stuck along the deep, narrow part.

"How is Man Gaac?" he said, again in English.

"She is at peace. I have brought word from her. She says, 'I want a paper.' She says you have not answered her letters."

Gac laughed. "Is she still working at the school?"

"Yes, she works hard there. She has much to do. Just now she is buying all the roofing grass to reroof the buildings with. I see her every day. She finds the money from me."

"It is good," he said. "I will send her a paper. When will you return back?"

"In three days," I told him.

"It is good," he said. "Next tomorrow I will come to you."

Gac was grinning all the time we talked. His face never became serious. What had once been an infectious smile now seemed to be a silly grin. He would raise his eyebrows, wrinkle his forehead, and laugh when there was nothing to laugh about. He never used to be this way.

He asked about the missionaries by name. He spoke always in English. "They are well," I said.

"How is Pastor Moses?"

"He is well. His wife is going to have a baby."

"That is good," he said.

"That woman of before," I asked, "is that your wife?"

"Yes," he said. He had been married once before, but his first wife died in childbirth the day before Christmas. I was in the hut with her, Man Gaac was there, too, and some other women. Man Gaac began to moan and to wail, then suddenly she stopped and spoke directly to the women: "That is the end. It shall not be repeated." And all was quiet.

"Do you like your work here?" I went on.

"Yes, I like it," he replied.

"Do the Arabs prohibit you from going to church?"

"No," he said, "we can go for one hour on Sundays."

"Do you go?"

"Sometimes. I am on the Christmas committee."

The sunlight was retreating out the door and only a small golden rectangle was left on the dark clay floor. "I will go now," I said, getting up to leave.

"It is so, my sister, I will come next tomorrow. I will bring something for Man Gaac. Go in peace, my sister," he said.

"*Uh,* remain in peace, my brother," I said.

Gac brought a bundle tied up in a cloth on the morning I was to leave, and a letter which I took home to his mother.

"How is Gac?" she asked me.

"He is well," I said.

"It is so," she said, happy again and not suspicious of anything. But then months went by with no further word from Gac. He'd been transferred, someone said who had come from Malakal. Gac did not write or send word to his mother about this. Finally, after many months a letter came, asking his mother for money. He needed it to buy food, he said. His salary should have covered that, but he did not explain himself. After that letter came another, and another, asking for money.

One day I heard her voice outside my door. "Do I come?" she said.

"*Uh,* come old mother," I answered from where I sat at my table working. The veranda door banged shut. The house door squeaked on its hinges. She strode across the room behind me, through the doorway and stopped at the old wicker chair where she sat down under the picture of a golden grain field, framed by purple mountains, which hung slightly crooked on a nail in the soft, brick wall.

I looked up from my papers. "Is it peace, old mother?" I said in the usual greeting, immediately aware that something was wrong.

"No," she said, "there is no peace." Her face was troubled. A sadness filled it.

"I have trouble, Nyarial," she said. Her voice could be very loud and strong, but today its strength was gone. "It is a big trouble." She studied her hands. There was a sore on one of them, probably a thorn. She picked at it with her finger, holding it so that the light from the big window would strike it. She was engrossed in her thoughts.

"What is the matter?" I asked.

"It is Gac," she said, clasping her hands in her lap and sitting back in the chair. I waited for her to go on. "He has broken his leg."

"Who did you hear it from?"

"His wife came on the boat from Malakal. She told me."

"What happened?"

"It is said he had a fight with another man. They were on the top of a boat in Malakal. Gac jumped down. That is what broke his leg."

"But why did his wife come back? Why did she not stay to help him?"

"Because Gac was put out of the police," she said.

"Why?" I asked, unable to understand how this could be.

"It is said he was drunk," she said, scarcely moving her lips.

We both sat there for a little while, saying nothing. I could think of quite a few young men who had been to school, gone to the town and floundered. It was a part of Progress. There were no delinquents in the village, only in the town, but neither was there progress. Progress was a foreign god, and these young men were being offered up to it in sacrifice. The world says: Don't stay in the village. Don't be primitive. Be educated. Be a leader. Yes, and we missionaries are a part of that urging, pressing, sophisticated world. But now, what happens to this boy? Who will pick him up out of the ditch? Who will explain to Man Gaac what has happened to her son? Will this become the pastor's responsibility too?

She comes to me. But suppose she goes to Kuac. What is he to say?

Man Gaac spoke again. "Nyarial," she said, "do you think God has cut him off?" There were tears in her eyes—tears of an African mother for her son. I had never seen an African cry for this reason before. But I understood this kind of weeping, and for the moment we were united together again—as on the day of her younger son's initiation, when the knife cut into his forehead and she looked away—united in our helplessness: the common ground of all humanity where one knows he needs a Savior.

There were many questions about God for which I had no answers, but to this one I could say something. "Old mother," I said, "do you remember the talk of God, at the place where it says a young man took the things his father gave him and went away to the town. He went and lived with a bad kind of living and lost everything he had and his heart was very sad. Then one day he came back home and his father went out to meet him and brought him food and gave him a cloth and a ring for his finger. Do you remember that?"

"*Uh,* I know it," she said.

"I think the important thing about that story is that the father of the boy stayed at home and waited for his son to return; and when the boy did return, his father accepted him. Now God is like this boy's father. He waits for us. And you, while you are still on this earth, must wait for Gac. God has love to give us so that we can wait for people like Gac. You will find this love from God.

"The love of God is a power we know only a very little bit. God says in His talk that nothing can conquer it. He says this because He and love are one. It cannot be said that Gac will return to a good way. This is not shown to us. It is the love of God which is shown to us. This is our comfort. Gac is on God's head—Gac is God's responsibility."

"It is so, Nyarial," she said. "We must pray." And she bowed her head and said:

"Old father, we call you now, we the people of sin. We are in trouble, old father. You, chief, help us. Gac is in trouble, old father. It is a big trouble. But you are the one with power. Help Gac in the house of magic at Malakal. Let your heart be soft toward him. He broke his leg. Help him, old father. We are calling you with the name of your son, Jesus."

Then she went away, out the door, out the gate, and back to her duties at the school.

13

WILL HE GIVE HER A STONE?

The Nuer people were undernourished. Their bodies were full of disease: tuberculosis, amoeba, malaria, yaws, to name a few. As Christians and followers of Jesus who "went about doing good" whether or not He was thanked, or understood, or believed, the need to help these people medically was inescapable to us.

With the introduction of medicine, however, we were faced with how to help the Nuer distinguish between what we were trying to do for the body and for the soul.

I had always heard that "medicine opens doors for the Gospel." This may be true, but in that it solves problems, it introduces how many others? If the Gospel is "simple" as some insist, it becomes complex by the "means" we use to draw men to it, and the African pastor inherits our complex Gospel. I spent much of my time talking with the people, and I recall one incident in particular which defined this puzzle for me.

The rain was pelting down on the steeply pitched thatch. Meer, a young woman whose name meant "tears," lay awake on the clay floor of her hut worrying about her little girl beside her. A soiled muslin mosquito net covered both of them like a blanket. It was early morning. Usually Meer would have been up and outside by this time, but as long as it rained no one stirred.

It was warm inside the hut and dark. A thick grass mat covered the tiny entrance.

Meer's little girl coughed, then spit and rubbed the spittle into the floor with her fingers. Fear rose in Meer's heart. She pulled the mat open a crack. "Is there blood still?" she said.

"They are few," the child answered, using the plural pronoun because liquids were always spoken of in the plural.

Meer lay back again listening to the persistent coughing of the child. She wished the rain would stop. She must milk the cow and take the milk to the doctor's house to be cooked there for Nyaliaa. The rain droned on. Questions marched through her mind. Would Nyaliaa live, or would she die like the rest? The last child had died in the rains; would Nyaliaa die then too? What does God want? Who has done the wrong? Why is He killing my children?

Another woman and her child were sleeping in the hut, too. The child sat up. Meer turned on her side to see.

"What is it?" his mother said.

"I go to urinate," he answered. He pushed aside the rag covering him and crawled to the doorway. Meer untied the grass rope securing the mat and the boy went out.

The rain had lessened and was falling very softly against the thatch. The sun was breaking through the layer of gray clouds along the horizon. Meer sat up, reached for the milk bucket, and crawled out the doorway. "I am going to milk the cow, my daughter," she said.

It was chilly enough outside to make Meer hug her naked breast and walk quickly to the barn, leaving her deep footprints outlined in the mud. The barn, like the hut, was made of sticks and mud. Meer stepped over the doorsill made of a V-shaped tree branch sunk in the ground. Inside, the air was warm and dry and smelled of smoke from the dung fire of the night before. Above her head dusty cobwebs were formed into lacy festoons on the thatch. Behind her, stuck above the door, was a small bunch of grass tied together like an old bouquet. This was the *wal,* the family magic, the word the people used for our medicine and for the clinic, the "house of magic."

"It is you, Meer?" said a man sitting Buddha-fashion in the raised circle of ashes in the center of the barn.

"*Uh,*" Meer said, glancing toward the man who had slept there in the warm ashes the night before, and was rubbing his teeth with his fingers, cleaning them with the ashes he had cupped in the palm of his hand.

"You have come to milk?" he said.

"*Uh,*" Meer answered as she walked along the mud wall behind the cattle to get her cow. The animals faced the center like spokes in a hub. They were separated by the poles holding up the roof. The man got up and came over to where Meer was untethering her cow. He rubbed his hand familiarly over the animal's bony rump and said, "You, go out. Go out." Lifting its head awkwardly over the back of the next animal, the cow pivoted slowly on its back legs and began going toward the barn doorway. The man kept his hand on the cow's rump, clucking to the animal with his tongue, encouraging its progress. At the oval entrance to the barn, the cow twisted its head, maneuvering its widespread horns through the mudded doorway without touching the wall on either side.

"How is your daughter?" the man said to Meer when the cow was safely outside.

"She is present still," Meer said. "I took her to the house of magic yesterday."

"It is good," he said. "God is present. Perhaps she will live."

"*Uh,* it is God's talk," Meer said resignedly, giving the standard reply.

Meer tethered the cow again outside the barn and, squatting down beside it, with one leg up and the other angled toward the ground, took hold of one teat and began stripping it with the thumb and forefinger of both hands, into the bucket. A milk gourd, she thought, would have been better. She could have held its narrow neck in the heel of her hand up against the teat and milked right into the opening. As it was the bucket seemed so far away, balanced on her knee. But the doctor's wife had insisted she must use this bucket. The white people are strange people. A tiny stream of milk dribbled down Meer's hand and over her thick bracelet. Flies began coming and the cow flicked its tail into Meer's face. "What is it?" she exclaimed indignantly. "Stand still."

There was a little less than two cups of milk in the bucket when she got up and walked back to the hut. That was all the cow produced.

Meer's little girl sat huddled against the side of the hut, wrapped in the old mosquito net, warming herself in the sun that was now showing. She was about eight years old and very thin. She said nothing as her mother went into the hut and came out again with a black cloth over her short *pac* (skirt) and the milk bucket in her hand. Picking up a small, doughnut-shaped grass ring from under the overhanging thatch, Meer put it on the patch of tightly curled ringlets crowning her head, and set the bucket on top. Now her head and body moved as one piece, as though they were welded together at her shoulders.

"Sit well, my daughter," she said, "I am going to the 'fenced-place,'" which was the word the people had given to the mission because it once had had a barbed-wire fence around it. "I will go and come," she said. "I will bring your milk from the house of the doctor." She used the Arabic word for doctor. "Perhaps God will cause your body to live."

The child sat very still, saying nothing. She watched her mother go. Suddenly Meer turned and called back, "Nyaliaa."

"*Uh,*" the little girl answered in a high, thin voice.

"My daughter, keep watching the goats well. If they go into the field, call Gatluak to chase them. He is in the barn. Do you hear?"

"*Uh,*" she answered.

The sky was heaped with white clouds sailing free. The dark rain clouds were gone, shoved away to the northern horizon where they would soon disappear. Meer's toes dug easily into the soft mud as she walked along the path, through the newly sprouted grain fields now soggy from the rain. She was a stranger here. Her village was three nights' sleeping across the river in a thorn forest by a small swamp. There were no foreigners there; she had never seen white people before. Now she was where they were, looking at their large brick houses ahead of her, and at their trees with fruit on them. *Lemun* (lay-moon) trees, they were called. Maybe she could find a *lemun* today. They were good to eat. Sour, she thought, and the saliva ran freely in her mouth.

Ahead of her was a woman carrying a baby basket on her head. She was making her way carefully over the slippery ground with an even-paced stride, while waving the gourd rattle in her right hand in concert with the crying baby in the basket. Meer adjusted her own pace to the woman's and followed behind, rehearsing to herself the events of the previous day. She had gone to the clinic for the first time in her life, and taken Nyaliaa. There were many people there. They had all sat out under the tree, waiting for the doctor. She recalled again the doctor's words and her response—When he said to me, "What is it?" I sat silently. The next man with the blind boy said, "He's talking to you. Tell him."

I said, "Child." I took my daughter's hand and made her get up for him to touch.

"She is dying," I said. Then he asked me her name. I told him.

"What is sore with her?" he asked.

"She has a cough," I said. Then he asked me when it began, but I did not hear him. I did not know he would ask so many questions. She is dying. I thought that was all he had to know. I thought he would give her life. I was tired of his questions. He asked me again, and the people sitting there said, "Woman there, he is asking you, 'When did it start?' Tell him." So then I remembered when it started; it was in the dry season, at the cattle camp. Her body became hot, I told him. Then he put a thing, a very thin thing, into her mouth and said, "Close your mouth." It was a thing of life, I think. Nyaliaa closed her mouth. He said, "Don't bite it." Nyaliaa held it well in her mouth. That is when I said to him, "Doctor, let my daughter live with the life of God."

He did not answer me. He asked another question, "Does the saliva have blood?" I said they were few. Then he took my child's arm and touched it. That was very good. He was giving her life, I think. He looked at her eyes. He is an important person, a big chief. Then he took the thing out of her mouth and looked at it, but he said nothing. He just gave me a paper thing and said, "Bring the child's saliva in this the day after tomorrow. When she wakes up she will spit saliva into this, then you will bring it."

He asked for the money. I gave it to him. It was tied up in my cloth. He did not ask for anything else. He said, "Go inside." The house was full of people. We sat down. We waited. We waited. It was a long time. There was a white girl, who called Nyaliaa's name, saying, "Come." I got up, and my daughter, and we went into another house. The white girl was tall. She had a paper. She said she had a plan for Nyaliaa. My heart was glad to hear this. It is the plan of God, I think. I heard a man talking about God while I was sitting under the tree. He said God gives people life. That is good. That is what I want for Nyaliaa. I am happy that I came to the house of magic.

The white girl said, "You will milk the cow. You will bring the milk to the house of the doctor. The milk will be cooked and other food will be mixed with it, then you will take it home to your daughter. Her body will become strong."

I liked that talk. It is good talk, truly. The plan of the white people is the plan of God. Tomorrow I will take the paper back to the house of magic. Nyaliaa will drink the magic there, and her blood will be good and she will live.

Meer was happy as she reached the clay road which ran behind the mission property. Puddles of water lay in the ditches. A flock of egrets, brilliantly white against new shoots of green grass, busied themselves hunting for food. She was encouraged to think that her child would live. The white people were very great, she thought as she swept her eyes across the buildings and water towers and fruit trees which she did not understand, but which was what made them great. This is what gave their God such power. Or was it that because their God was great they had this power? She did not know. In fact, she did not reason it through. It was simply that what appeared in front of her eyes proved to her that both they and their God were very great.

She turned onto the brick path which paralleled the river and went past the doctor's house. A little boy came toward her, leading his blind grandmother. "Go slowly, my child," the old woman said, "the path is very bad." The brick path of the foreigner was strange to her and unfamiliar to her feet. The little boy said nothing. He did not look back toward the worried face. He had not the sense nor the worries of an old blind person.

At the doctor's bungalow Meer paused for a moment in front of the glass windows of the bedroom and smiled. She crossed over the brick edging of the path onto the grass in front of the house to get closer to the window, and then stood there, watching curiously at the expressions which kept changing on her face. She grinned grandly, showing her two buck teeth. She stuck out her tongue. She pulled back her cloth and rubbed her hand slowly over her body. She turned her head with the can of milk on it and laughed quietly to herself. Voices coming on the path made her move quickly away to the screen door where she stopped.

She clapped her hands together and called through the screen, "Is there a person in the house?"

No answer.

Flies bit at her ankles. She rubbed one foot against the other. The metal bangles on her legs clinked together. She pressed her nose flat against the screen hoping to catch sight of someone on the inside. Instead she saw a doll lying as if asleep on the inner window ledge. She stood transfixed, and was presently joined by the houseboy who, hearing her call, had finished washing the dishes first before coming to the door. Now he stood in front of her on the opposite side of the screen, wiping his hands on a dingy apron.

"What is it, Meer?" he said.

"That," she said, "what is it?"

Tuut, who delighted in demonstrating the white man's novelties, had already followed her gaze to the doll and was ready to pick it up when she asked the question. He brought it over to the screen, cuddling it in his long, black arms, its pink body resting clumsily against him. Knowing how the doll worked he was very careful to keep it in a horizontal position so that Meer would see it well. Then he tilted it upright, causing its eyes to open, and held it out at her.

All that was in Meer froze in fear. *"Ay! Ay!"* she cried, drawing back. Tuut, amply rewarded, caught his breath in frequent gasps, until he could hold it in no longer and burst out into a loud *Ayow*, and collapsed onto the screen ledge. Meer had advanced cautiously to the screen again, but would step away each time Tuut's movements caused the doll to open or close its eyes. Finally, driven by her curiosity, she opened the door and walked into the house. Approaching the doll with some reserve she put out her hand to touch it. Tuut thrust it at her so that she ran away. "It will eat you," he said loudly, then doubled up again in a fit of laughter.

"What is it, Tuut? Is it a thing of God?" she said from a distance.

And Tuut, well informed and always sure of himself, said, "No, it is not a god, it is a clay figure."

"Is it living?" Meer asked when the eyes fell shut again.

"No, of course not," he said, pleased at his own confidence.

"Whose is it?"

"It belongs to the white people."

"*Ah,* the white people, they are gods," she said.

Dhoaal, Meer's husband, had also come to us, seeking help for his sick daughter. He was a hard-working, imaginative man with a few graying hairs. He had large hands with bony knuckles which he used freely when he talked, and a chronically swollen knee which pained him when he walked or knelt or hoed in his field. Still this did not keep him from going on long journeys or hoeing a large field.

Dhoaal came to our house at odd hours, announcing himself by clapping as he walked in. He would come around to the veranda, sit down on the old, green laundry box and there repeat in the most solemn manner how ill he had been and how he had recovered. "Look," he would say, "before, I was down on the ground, my body had no more strength. Now I am living." He stuttered in his earnestness. "It was as though I had died. But I came to the house of magic, and look, I lived," he would say, looking down at himself very pleased. "God helped me, truly. It is true, my sister, it has gone into my heart. The God Jesus, He is God."

He would pause, then if his audience could spare the time, he would go on. "Before, I was a prophet of the people. Now I have left it. Now I kill the snakes. I hit them on the head with my stick. I hit them. I hit them until they die." He would snap his forefinger against his middle finger in rapid succession, simulating the crack of the stick on the snake's head. "I have no fear, my sister. The people say, 'You will die. You will truly die.' No, I will not listen to their talk." He would flick the back of his ear with his forefinger, indicating that their words passed him by unheeded. Then he would laugh.

"It is like that," he would say with the earnestness of a judge, "and because of it I have come here to stay by you white people, and the house of magic. And now, my daughter, she is sick. I have had many troubles before, but now I have come to you. Look. These five," he would say, lifting his right hand for me to see and closing his fingers down into a fist beginning with the thumb—one, two, three, four, five—"all of them are dead. My five children, they are in the ground." He would point to the floor and click his tongue against the roof of his mouth, confirming what he had said. "Now my little girl is sick. She is the sixth one. There are no more. I told my wife to bring her. She will live because of you. I told her, 'You will go to Nyarial. She will tell you the talk of God.'"

"Why have you not told her?" I asked him.

"My sister, I always tell her, but it is a hard talk. It does not go into her heart. If you will tell her maybe it will reach her heart."

The plain was green with standing grain ripening in the sun. The broad green leaves faced me liked crossed swords as I walked into them. They brushed harshly against my face and arms and rustled in my ears, reminding me of the white-veined leaves of the corn in the fields back home.

The drab-colored cones of thatch on the huts and barns topped the grain, and both the cones and the grain pointed to the brilliant sky with its great pillars of cloud so white and clean. The ground in the grain fields was drying out, crusting and beginning to crack. I walked along beside the path and could feel the spongy ground spring under my feet. It felt good. I was on my way to visit Meer.

Meer had been with us for over three months and had come faithfully each day, bringing the milk and taking it back again for her little girl. She had come to church, too, and had come often to talk. Meer never saw me without saying that she wanted God to give life to her daughter. And always when she said it my heart sank. Life for the body and life for the soul were one and the same thing to Meer. I had said to her, "Meer, has it not gone into your heart that the life of God is not for the body of a person, it is for the *breath* of a person?" I wanted to say spirit, but spirit and breath were the same word. There was no distinction. Meer just smiled.

"Is breath present with you, Meer?"

"*Uh,* it is present," she said.

"How do you know?"

"I don't know," she said.

"Because you are living. When a person dies his breath goes out of him, as the people say. It leaves the body. Don't you see?"

"*Uh,* it is so. It is so. That is what I want. I want the breath of God," she said.

"Jesus said He would give us life, Meer, but not life for the body. He meant life for the breath of a person." Meer looked blank, then smiled, then looked worried again.

"My sister," she said, "all of my children are dead." She held up her fist. "Five of them. They are in the ground. If only my daughter were injected she might live."

"Meer, that is not it. You cannot trust the magic of the white people. It is not to be trusted in. It is not God. The magic of the white people does not give life to the breath of a person.

"But the doctor," she said, "he has five children, he and his wife, and they do not die."

"*Uh,* I know it. That is true," I said, thinking of all the medical care those children had had, and their father a doctor, their mother a nurse.

"It is God's talk," Meer said conclusively, ending the conversation. It was the inevitable answer, the one always given, not just by Meer, by everyone. What did it mean? It meant whatever happens, life or death, good or evil—all of it is God's doing. He controls everything. And they were right. Man could not make the sun to shine, or bring the rain. He could not cause barren women to conceive, or keep a child alive. These four basic needs he could not meet.

As I walked along under the thick tops of white grain, I thought of how in civilized countries we had challenged God. From granaries to safety belts we had made it our business to protect ourselves from death. We spent our lives trying to outfox death, to keep it as far out of our lives as possible. So our understanding of God was very sophisticated. We had little reason to consider Him in connection with our physical well-being. We could take care of ourselves. Those of us who did consider Him more personally than others could hardly base the fact of being adequately clothed, for example, on an earnest consideration of the lilies of the field that they neither sew nor spin, subsequently to discover that our heavenly Father had seen to it that we had got the clothes we wore. No, we hadn't put that to the test.

And food. If whether or not we ate depended on the harvest, we would have to *reckon* with God, not only worship Him. As it was we didn't have to reckon much with God in order to live. At least I didn't. I could evade Him if I wanted to. I could come to terms with daily living so long as I had money, or credit, and didn't think too seriously.

Their knowledge of God came from nature. Mine came from a Book. There had to be this Book, else how would anyone have known that "God is love"? Or that God revealed Himself in Jesus

Christ? But the Nuer never had this Book. That is, they never had the revelation. But they did have God and death. They have always had this. It is the *revelation* they have never had.

More and more I was coming to realize that between the two of us, Meer had had to face reality more than I. She had to face suffering. Like her people she was schooled in suffering and regardless of what happened, I knew she would not collapse.

I walked out of the cool, shaded grainfield into Meer's hot, clay yard and found her, legs straight as she bent over from the waist to sweep the yard with a small grass broom. She saw me and, dropping the broom, put her hands on her hips, cocked her head to one side, and smiled happily. Her short, black *pac* hung halfway to her knees, and above it she was bare. I walked up to her and shook her hand.

"Is it peace, my sister?" I said.

"*Uh.* It is peace. You have come?"

"*Uh,* I have come."

The sun was shining out of the west, shining with unrelenting penetration from a great height above the horizon into the very marrow of one's bones. We walked the few paces to the hut. Meer stooped down and pulled *out* the stiff sleeping skin which leaned against the hut wall, tapped it with her hand to dust it off, then put it on the ground for us both to sit on.

"Sit," she said. Nyaliaa was also sitting by the hut. Her hands were curled in her lap. The nails of her fingers were long, too long for those of an active child. Her chest looked like a washboard, small ribs evenly spaced covered with thin, black skin. Her lips were dry and chapped and stuck against her upper front teeth.

"Nyaliaa, are you at peace?" I greeted her.

"*Uh,*" she said, scarcely speaking.

"Here. Take these," I said, handing her the two limes I had brought with me. She took them hesitantly, putting one in her lap, and the other she began to peel, then to suck noisily.

"Why did you not bring me one, Nyarial?" Meer said, looking at me sheepishly.

"Do you like limes, Meer?" I asked, teasing her.

Nyaliaa began to cough. She got up, clutching the unpeeled lime. Meer watched her quizzically. "Where are you going?" she said.

"I am going into the hut," the little girl answered.

I watched the thin ankles go past me and the narrow, bony feet. "Her cough is still? It is not better?" I said.

"*Uh,* she is dying, Nyarial. If she dies, I die too. What shall I do?"

The sun, shining behind us, sent a stream of light along the side of Meer's kind, troubled face. To her, anything other than life for her child was like giving her a stone when she had asked for bread. If Meer was to live, life must come through her child, for if the child were to die, she would be divorced. She had told me this herself. Yes, and the tongues of the women will wag, and they will say, "Meer, the daughter of Tay, the wife of Dhoaal, do you know, she is divorced? Her six children, all of them are dead." They will gaze down the long wooden stems of their charcoal pipes, and spit into the dust, these women who form an exclusive sisterhood, whose claim to membership is a living child. Thus the news will travel until the men know, the women know, the boys and girls know . . . until everyone knows that Meer, the daughter of Tay, the wife of Dhoaal, had six children, all of whom died, and she is divorced, and no man wants her. And Meer will become like a dog going about hunting a child.

Death can often be avoided with proper care. But to get this across defeated me. I looked around that yard. How could one fight tuberculosis in this setting, for this is what Nyaliaa had. If cleanliness and sterility are components of a cure, then there is no hope. How can one sterilize water and keep it that way in a clay pot? How does one cope with flies in a cattle country where flies are legion? How does one insist on the use of soap when the cost is prohibitive?

"How many cattle have you killed to God?" I said.

She looked down at her hands and began to count, beginning with the thumb, folding it into her palm. "Five," she said, naming each animal, and ticking off five different days of hope in her life which eventually faded and died.

Instinctively, I turned again to the words of Scripture. I leaned heavily on them. I trusted God to make them meaningful to Meer. I had in mind to quote to her John 3: 16, because I knew she knew it. She had learned it at the clinic prayer time. But first I said, "Did you find life when you killed those cattle, Meer?"

She shook her head. "No."

I was at the edge of a precipice, where I would have to leap from the terra firma of the physical world into the intangible spiritual world, where I knew she could not come unless God gave her understanding. "Meer," I said, "you know this talk, now listen to it again." I quoted her the verse in the Nuer language, thinking the words to myself in English as I spoke. The words sounded wonderful to me. My hand was outstretched, pointing into the air, as I emphasized the parts most pertinent to her in her trouble. I longed to explain it to her; surely it showed on my face. But Meer sat there, her hands in her lap, her troubled face drawn up in a combination of worry and fear.

Finally she said, "Nyarial, will Jesus make my daughter live?"

We were back on terra firma again. That is, I was. Meer had never left it.

"I do not know, Meer," I said, searching her face, which was veiled with the sorrow that clung to her so often.

"Has it not gone into your heart, yet, Meer?"

"No," she said quietly, "it has not gone into my heart."

I relaxed against the mud wall of the hut, helpless. Lord, is she part of the harvest? Am I a reaper? Is the message for her? How is she to know it? What will make her understand? It's not that someone needs to be "sent." It's not that she needs a "preacher." It's that she can't *hear.*

All the way home along the narrow footpath, I pondered what I had said to Meer. John 3:16, supposedly the simple Gospel. But what had she heard? I thought of the words—the way in which she probably had understood them.

God . . . *the one who kills her children* . . . loved all the people so much . . . *how could that be true, He kills people* . . . that He gave his one only son . . . *but she had given Him five children already . . .* so that the person who believes Him will not die . . . *but how could this be, even the white man dies* . . . but will live with life which does not end . . . *who wants to keep on living when life is so hard?*

Everywhere I looked over the countryside, nothing to be seen could endure for more than a few years. The houses and barns would fall down, eaten by termites. Even the straggly thorn trees would be gone, cut down by the Nuer's dull, crude ax. Only the ground would remain to be swept by the wind, pelted by the rain, baked hard by the sun. Meer and her people would walk over it, bury their children and be buried in it. How *were* they to know they had not been forsaken?

We at the mission prayed for Meer and her child. After the grain was harvested, the stocks cut down, and the plain was bare again, Meer took Nyaliaa home to her village. Some time later Dhoaal came in.

"How is Meer?" I asked him. "Has she come back yet?"

"No," he said, "she will not come back."

"What is it?" I said.

"The child has died."

"She died?"

"*Uh*. She died," he said, clicking his tongue in confirmation. "It is the talk of God."

"And you," I said, using the plural form, "what will you do, you and Meer?"

"It is said there will be a divorce."

"It is said by whom? Is it your talk?" I asked, meaning his talk alone.

"No, it is the talk of my people. My brother, he says it is on her head, the death of the child. He says that she will be divorced. It is God's doing, he says. But Meer's people, they say it is I. That the children die is my fault. They say, he will be divorced."

"What do you say?"

"What can I say, my sister?"

They were divorced.

I saw Meer for the last time some years later. I was walking along the path one day, conscious only of a blurred line of people coming toward me. Suddenly a woman stepped out of the line and stood in sharp focus in front of me. I prepared myself for some request: a coin, a cloth, hoping to make as charitable a negative reply as I dared without sacrificing the finality of my answer. The woman disarmed me by the simplicity of her attitude, and the expectancy in her voice when she looked at me with a grin and said, "Nyarial, do you know me?"

She looked strangely familiar in a dirty, black cloth, and there was something about the tilt of her head I recognized. I could not think for the moment who this was, but I felt drawn to her, as if there were something personal between us, and I wanted to remember. Her face relaxed into a patient smile as she waited for my reply while my mind raced wildly about in search of a name.

Then it came to me. "You are Meer!" I exclaimed.

"*Ah,* Nyarial," she beamed, "you know me. You know my name!" In that moment the past merged with the present. Meer, I thought, oh—what has happened to you? Your child? Is there one?

It would seem by the great smile on her face that she had never known trouble, or that if she had it was now forgotten. "My sister," I said, "is there a child?"

The smile on her face died, and I knew—she was still alone.

14

LIFE IS IN THE BLOOD

Medicine did not always fail. It sometimes brought spectacular results. This was gratifying to the missionary who thought of the miracles of medicine as a demonstration of the love of God. The blow came, however, when we realized that our medicine was engendering a false faith in God and the white man instead. Many times I talked with patients and their families trying to explain to them the love of God.

One day I stepped from the brilliant sunlight into the long patch of shade bordering the row of eucalyptus trees. The shade fell across the entrance to the maternity hut which sat by itself, away from all the other patients' huts. Ducking down I went inside.

Nyabieel was lying in a coma on a grass mat on the clay floor, close to the wall, and the others—her old mother, her brother, and the missionary nurse—were sitting by her. Away from them, to the back of the hut, was a tiny baby, loosely wrapped in a white flannel, its long legs the color and texture of thin frankfurters, and the bottoms of its thin feet a dainty pink.

Dangling from a small, plastic bag of blood tied to the thatch above Nyabieel was a transparent hose feeding the needle stuck in her right arm. The arm was bound to a board with white surgical gauze and rested, palm upward, on the dirt floor. The patient was a postpartum anemia victim, one of many, the majority of whom died. She was receiving the first blood transfusion to be given at Nasir. Her mother and brother sat as in a stupor with their gaze fixed, watching as she tossed her head from side to side, and gasped for breath, emitting strange gurgling sounds from her throat. Cloths she had formerly worn were now draped across the lower half of her body, and a piece of blue muslin was wound around her stomach, in keeping with the custom for new mothers. The rest of her body was bare. Her hair was plaited in strips like the Arab women's, and there was a flat, metal earring in each ear.

The hut was uncluttered except for a white enamel hospital tray on the floor, full of transfusion paraphernalia—a wad of cotton, an ampule and syringe, a kidney basin, and a large aluminum cooking pot with dry porridge crusted on its sides.

No one said anything when I came in and sat down; only their eyes moved. I nodded to the old mother, "Are you at peace, old mother?"

"*Uh*," she whispered automatically.

No, I thought, you are not at peace, old mother. You are afraid. You think Nyabieel is going to die, and your son thinks so too. I can tell by the looks on your faces, as you sit not moving, not making a sound, watching and waiting.

I, too, sat watching the blood. It was dropping in very slowly. A metal clamp on the hose controlled its flow. I wanted to open the clamp and let the blood flow. I felt if a little was good, more would be better, and frequent gaspings of the woman were persuading me that this blood was not going to get to her in time. I was not a nurse and I knew nothing about transfusions; I had never seen one before, but I did not want Nyabieel to die. I looked at my watch. Two thirty. It was at eight o'clock that morning when I was leaving the doctor's house that her husband, Jal, had come, calling him. He had tears in his eyes, which surprised me. I had never seen him before. He was a young man, a policeman; his face was fat and boyish-looking, and everything about him was neat and clean. He said his wife was dying, but I did not believe it. Everybody called "wolf" when there was none.

Nyabieel was a quiet, unassuming young woman in her early twenties who was baptized and came to the Bible class occasionally with her sister, a bold, flippant type of person by contrast, clever at Arab embroidery and cooking. Nyabieel's marriage was an especially profitable one because her husband had a salary and had been able to get the cows required for the marriage payment. Jal had also been the financial source for blankets and beads, mosquito nets and clothes and whatever Nyabieel's family had wanted. This was Nyabieel's first child and it seemed impossible that she should die. Others might die, but not Nyabieel. Oh, no. I did not know what to look for as a sign of recovery in a transfusion, but here I was beside her, looking at her on the mat, in a coma, muscles relaxed, her mouth drooling saliva, her brown eyes rolling back and forth, back and forth, her arms limp at her sides, her stubby, fanned-out toes pointing upward. She was more like a corpse than a person. I had told her husband not to worry, that the doctor would help her; now I was not so glib. What was needed was a miracle.

Turning to the nurse I blurted, "Is she going to make it? She looks dead to me." She lifted her eyebrows, signaling her contemplative mood.

"Well, I don't know," she said, "it's hard to say."

"Why does the blood have to drop in so slowly? She'll be dead before it finishes."

"This is the first transfusion we've ever given, you know. It's really an experiment and the thing is to learn how fast the blood should flow. I'm timing that now and later on might open the cock slightly. I'm afraid to let it go in too fast."

Oh, so that's it, it has to go slowly, I thought.

Drop . . . drop . . . drop . . . down the hose, now through the needle, and into the vein. Fantastic! How white her nails are. Oh blood, whatever you're supposed to be doing, do it. There's life in the blood, that's what I want to see. If only God would intervene. God? No, maybe He does not have much to do with it; it's the blood or nothing. Oh, how she flings that arm about. Hold it down, old mother . . . that's it.

The woman sat between her daughter and the wall, watching, anticipating every move the girl might make. The skin on her face was taut, drawn around her protruding front teeth as if pulled together by a drawstring.

Old mother, with your beads and bracelets on, I know what you're thinking. You are wondering whose mistake this is. Who made God angry . . . who has cursed your daughter. How far back do you search the past? Months, or years? I know, you are trying to understand why it has happened. I am trying to understand, too. But it is easier for me. Science tells me. You have no science. I understand that it has to do with the chemistry of her blood. The problem lies within her own body; it has nothing to do with anyone or anything outside. Science tells me that. But you don't know science. And even if you did, it would not bring you peace. Peace comes from God. The same God who is killing your daughter can give you peace, even if she dies. You may not feel it all the time, but it will be there. I believe this. It is what keeps me anchored to hope. Not hope that everything will be all right, but hope that all will be made right some day. But how can I say this to you, old mother? God is some kind of magic to you. You use His name as a talisman.

Jesus. Jesus, you will say with your hand lifted in supplication. You don't know who He is. I will tell you: He is the Son of God.

Yes, you say, that is true, God has many sons. How can I explain to you what I mean? Anyway, you have no word for hope even if you understood about Jesus.

I did not especially enjoy the silence and turned again to the nurse. "Who gave the blood for the transfusion?" I asked.

"Her husband and her brother here," she nodded toward the young man. "Amazing, isn't it?" she said, anticipating my thoughts. I looked above her head to the plastic bag hanging from the thatch. I thought to myself, they've never seen a transfusion before, and yet without any propaganda or demonstration, they willingly submit to giving their blood to someone else. No questions, no qualms apparently . . . that's fatalism. But what else do they know? If the witch doctor's magic does not work, try the white doctor's, his magic is stronger. If one God does not work, try another. It is no wonder Jesus and the white man have such a good reputation with penicillin and sulfa drugs to back them up . . . then too, they confuse spiritual life with physical life, but how can they help that when the word for spirit is also the word for breathing? If the sick person recovers it is said, "God let him live"; and if he dies, it is said, "God let him die," regardless of where he was treated or by whom. But we missionaries argue and say, if a person who was treated by us lives, it is the *love* of God, and if he dies (and only if he was treated by us) that it is God's *will*.

Drop . . . drop . . . drop . . . drop. The nurse opened the cock a trifle.

"Oh wonderful! That makes me feel better," I said. "She hasn't improved at all though, has she?" The nurse shook her head, no.

I shifted my leg to a more comfortable position. The mud floor was cool and firm against my skin. My back was tired. I wondered how much longer we would have to wait. It was a nice hut, though. It had just been finished. The mudded walls were smooth and clean. How can they make it like that, I thought. Women with rough, calloused hands, so unlike my own, had done it with their long, thin fingers, which were used to the pricks and jabs of the sharp slivers of dry grass they mixed with the mud to make the plaster. I had tried to do it once, but had come away with the palms of my hands stinging and the women laughing at me. It was hot working in the sun, with the sweat running in rivulets over their shiny, shaven heads, and around their eyes and down their chests and backs, and mud halfway up their arms.

The blood was at the quarter mark on the bag. Soon it would be empty, and following that . . . ?

The brother sat with his legs drawn up in front of him hugging his knees with his hands. He had on khaki shorts and a white shirt open at the neck. The sleeves were rolled up and the shirttail stuck out all around. He wore canvas shoes with no laces, tramped down at the heels as the Arabs wore their shoes. The holes in his earlobes were empty; there was no necklace around his neck and no bracelets on his arms or legs. Instead he wore a wristwatch with a white plastic band. It showed the time at twenty minutes after ten. He had let his hair grow and had shaved a part on one side. He was an advanced schoolboy, home from government school on holiday and was negotiating with one of the schoolgirls' fathers at the mission to marry his daughter. He had visited the girls' school, as well, showing unusual interest in the well-being of the students and particularly in the one he was interested in marrying. He had distinguished himself by advising the headmistress that students should not be expected to do school chores and they should be fed Arab food, instead of the local variety they now ate.

Now he faced the future in a different light. If his sister died the cattle paid for her would be returned, leaving him no cattle with which to pay for his wife. He sat darkly, in the gloom of his own predicament, watching with the greatest attention the strange, restless movements of his sister, sharpening his focus and alerting himself to the possibility of her final breath with each strenuous gasp she made.

The gradual dripping of the blood continued. It seemed a futile way to expect to alleviate the frequent, forceful, desperate gaspings of the woman, and to satisfy the cravings of her body which, dispossessed of its senses, wrestled grotesquely for oxygen.

But suddenly, with no forewarning, she began to move her lips, trying to speak. The old mother, keenly sensitive to the signs of both life and death, bent down close to the girl's face and called, "Nyabieel. Nyabieel. Who am I?"

Her eyes fluttered and changed from a cold stare to a steady, intelligent gaze; her breathing resumed its regular quiet rhythm. The old woman spoke again. Deliberately turning her head, the girl looked at all of us, then back to her mother. Softly, her lips scarcely meeting, she said, "It is you, old mother."

I laughed aloud with joy. "She truly lives, old mother," I said. I looked up at the bag; the blood was almost gone. It had saved her life.

The next day the baby Nyabieel had borne died, but the people did not mourn. As long as the mother survived, more children would follow.

Some days later Nyabieel was able to leave the maternity hut and go home. The times one would greet her with "Are you at peace? How is your body?" became less and less as she grew stronger and resumed her daily chores.

Then after the season had changed and the rains had begun, on a pleasant afternoon, following a morning of heavy showers, I went to visit Nyabieel and her mother in the village. Her husband was on duty at a post along the Ethiopian border. She had not been able to join him since her recovery because the road had been closed due to the beginning of the rains, and the river had not yet risen high enough for the province steamers to travel on it. It was rumored now that a boat was on its way and would be going as far as the government border station.

The cornstalk fence around the hut and yard was no longer there. It had been used up gradually for the cooking fires each day and only the jagged edges, where it had been broken off close to the ground, remained. The hut was old and tumbledown, with a decided sag on one side and the thatched roof, soggy from the rain, sat strangely on it.

Spread out on a mat on the ground in front of the hut was some sprouted grain for making beer, drying in the sunshine, and along the side and to the back of the hut, half hidden under the over-hanging thatch skirt of the roof, were large, carbon-crusted clay pots used for brewing beer. Nyabieel's mother made and sold beer for a living as did many other women living near the government and army quarters. It was the only sure, quick way for a woman to earn money in this land, except for prostitution, a profession open exclusively to barren women.

Three skinny, prickly-necked chickens were pecking near the grain, and I knew someone would be close by keeping an eye on them.

"Are you at peace?" I called. "Is there someone in the house?"

"*Uh,* we are at peace," said a voice from inside. I walked up to the black, oval opening in the side of the hut as Nyabieel's mother leaned around the entrance, her pipe in her hand and said, "It is you, Nyarial?"

"*Uh,* it is I, old mother," I said, identifying myself in the age-old greeting, and she smiled a welcome to me showing a broken front tooth, and I stooped and went in.

"*Ah,* you chickens, move yourselves," she called out at the pecking hens as I greeted Nyabieel who was sitting on a bed which sagged in the middle and was propped up on a five-gallon tin at one end.

"Are you present, Nyabieel? Are you at peace?" The greeting was especially appropriate for this woman who had so recently brushed with death. The greeting had grown out of the people's need for an affirmation of their struggle against death.

"*Uh,* it is peace," she said, giving me her hand. Her mother did the same, lightly grasping my fingers by the second knuckles and letting them go after one shake. Then she settled back against the wall and spat into the yard, only to notice the chickens back in the grain again.

"*Ah*, you bad chickens," she cried, giving the ground a loud crack with a piece of cornstalk that was lying beside her, which sent the chickens flying, "will you finish all of them?"

The hut was full of things: a table, the bed, sacks of grain, old packing boxes, cooking gourds and bowls, a five-gallon can holding a lantern with a broken chimney, and a new piece of "Camel" soap with the imprint of the camel raised distinctly in the center of it.

The old woman began to talk. "It was the blood," she said very earnestly, looking at me. "The doctor is a very clever man. He took the blood from her husband," and she nodded at Nyabieel, "and put it in her. It was in a little bag that had a long arm that had a needle [she used an adaptation of the Arabic word for needle] in its mouth. I asked Jal, 'Did it hurt?' He said, 'No, it did not hurt.' The blood went in—teck, teck, teck," she said skipping her finger to indicate each drop, "very slowly. It was big work. I saw it with my eyes."

She took her pipe from against the wall and sucked into the mouthpiece. There was no fire in it, so she hunted around in an old gourd beside her for a few bits of charcoal to put in the pipe bowl at the end of the long wooden stem. Assiduously arranging the lumps of charcoal with her thumb and forefinger, she presently satisfied herself that the air was coming through and the charcoal would burn, and looked up to say, "Ah, you white people, you are gods!" Then she picked a hot coal out of a smaller gourd behind her, held it lightly in her fingers and arranged it on top of the charcoal in the pipe.

She sucked long and hard until the lighted coal glowed an orange-red and began igniting the bits next to it. She sucked more rapidly, and the heated air she drew into her mouth made her spit, arcing a stream of saliva neatly out the door. Again she saw the chickens, and again she cried out, "Ah, those chickens. They repeat themselves! What will I do? Nyabieel, my daughter, go, chase them."

Nyabieel ducked out, clapping her hands at the chickens, sending them in all directions, and inside the old woman went back to her pipe, sucking on it furiously, to make sure it was burning well. She was in no hurry to make conversation.

She sat back and stretched one leg out in front of her, keeping the other one bent up in front of her face. It was a long, shiny, thin leg with a wrinkled callous patch on the knee.

I thought perhaps she had said all she was going to say about Nyabieel and her sickness, but she began again: "These white people, they are truly God." She emphasized the word *truly* and looked straight at me. I had heard this countless numbers of times from the people. They often said it after the doctor had saved a life, and I heard it once at the airstrip when, after the plane took off, a naked villager turned to his companion and said, incredulously, "These white people, they are God!" But as for Nyabieel's mother, here on the floor in front of me, with her pipe in her hand, her short, tight-fitting skirt around her, her flabby breasts and thin but tough-soled feet, *she* had witnessed a miracle. That she attributed it to the white man was correct, and that she therefore called him God was logical. But what was I to say?

"The white man is clever, old mother," I said, "but he is not God, only Jesus is God." (The name "Jesus" was almost impossible for a Nuer to pronounce, so we called him Jitheth, the closest approximation to it.)

The fact that Jesus was on earth as a man only made it easier for her to believe that other men might also be gods, since the things some of them did were, in her eyes, as miraculous as the tales she heard about Jesus.

"*Uh*, Jesus. Jesus." She lifted her hands ceremoniously into the air. "Jesus is a good God. Jesus is a great God. Jesus is the God of the white people." She took her pipe again and sucked into the metal mouthpiece, disturbed to see that the fire was not burning well.

"Yes," I answered, "Jesus is the God of the white people, but my mother, He is also God of the people of the world."

"*Uh*," she said, "He is the God of the white people, and the black people, and the brown people." Those were all the kinds of people she knew—Europeans, Africans, and Arabs. "He is a good God," she said again as a refrain, and sat back in her own little world, puffing her pipe, separated centuries from me.

I thought the woman was greatly confused, and I shared in her confusion. Medicine, I reflected, and the doctor's skill had caused her to see a miracle, a "work which amazes the people," as the Nuer says. Even as divine power had enabled Mary and Martha to see "the glory of God," as Jesus promised them, at the raising of their brother, Lazarus, from the dead. The experience for Mary and Martha had strengthened their faith in Jesus that He was the Christ, the Son of God, and it also caused "many of the Jews" to "believe on Him." Fortunately, Jesus *was* God and His methods *were* divine. Unfortunately, the mission doctor was a man, and his methods human. But how was the old woman to know that what she saw was not the direct glory of God? How was she to know that the doctor, a simple man even as Jesus was a simple man to Mary and Martha, was not God?

If we insist to her and to all of the countless others like her, that our medicine and its effects witness to God's love, and if we connect in any way God's name to our medicine, then we must be ready to accept the appraisal of the Nuer of who we are, that is, that we are gods. If we insist that missionary medicine does show forth the glory and love of God, then we must consider whether medical cures everywhere are not also of God, and acknowledge that cures we attribute to prayer alone *do* occur elsewhere without prayer, or through the prayers of Hindus, Muslims, and pagan rituals.

I knew of no way to clarify the issue for the old woman and turned to Nyabieel who had come back into the hut. She was sitting on the floor churning some milk in a gourd. "Is your body strong now, Nyabieel?" I said.

"*Uh*, I am well now, my body is good," she said with a shy smile. "I am going away. I am going to Jal."

"Are you going on the steamer?"

"*Uh*." She rocked the gourd back and forth on her leg, bouncing it up and down intermittently. The milk sloshed against the rough sides of the gourd. I was surprised to hear that she was going, forgetting for an instant that no place on the plains differed from another to any extent. A hut was a hut, and a woman cooked and carried water the same way in one place as another. There would be no doctor, but a doctor was a luxury and not a necessity. Sickness and death were common parts of life, and were not to interfere with anyone's plans.

"You will go and stay for a long time?" I said.

"Next year, when Jal takes his leave, I will come."

"Do you want to go?" I asked. She must go, I knew, because it was expected of her to bear a child.

She shrugged her shoulders, "What else can I do?" she said, still rocking the gourd on her knee.

The nurse had told me that Nyabieel was not fully recovered in that her body had not resumed its normal functioning.

"Are you not afraid to go? What about your body, will it get better there?"

"I am not afraid," she said. "I will go to the doctor. He will give me medicine. I will take it with me. God will help me." She held the gourd still and smiled innocently. The old woman reached over and took the gourd to finish churning the milk. The product would not be butter; the weather was too warm. She took off the twisted leather cap and poured the buttery oil out into a tin cooking pot. Then she rubbed her oily hands over her legs making them shine.

"Nyarial," she said, "when Nyabieel goes to the house of magic tomorrow, she will stop at your house and you will give her a bottle for my oil." On the last word, she looked up from her rubbing to see the answer on my face.

The inevitable has happened, I thought to myself, she has made this visit profitable. "Yes, old mother, I will give it to her."

I left the hut and went home. I took the road through the government and merchants' quarters where square mud houses with thatched roofs stood in blocks between two dirt roads running the length of the post, paralleling the river. I walked by the jail where a line of prisoners in white muslin overblouses and pantaloons and white muslin hats filed through the gate, followed by a smartly dressed policeman with a gun over his shoulder. Being a prisoner was one of the best breaks the people got, for it meant wearing a uniform and being fed regularly each day, which they enjoyed.

A man passed me, leading a goat on a rope. Two small Arab boys in white *jelabeeyas*, which reached to their ankles, and wearing orange skullcaps ran ahead of me, pushing old bicycle wheels with cornstalks like hoops. Buxom Arab women stood in a cluster by the opening in a fence, chattering, their heads wrapped carelessly in black or white veils with their faces uncovered. When they saw me they called out in Nuer, "Nyarial, where did you go? Did you go to pray?"

I greeted them and smelled the heavy perfume which filled the air around them. I told them the news that Nyabieel was leaving on the boat. They knew she had been ill. "*Ah*, she was almost dead," one of them said. "The doctor gave her blood. Just like the hospital in Khartoum. You white people, you are good people, you are the people of God. God has helped her truly." I listened to them, amused. They were so like Western women in their ability to chat.

I told them the sun was small and I must go. They said, "Go in peace."

It would be well if this were the end of the story. At least one could be satisfied that a young woman's life had been saved through medicine. But the story continues, and it must stop with the last word I had of Nyabieel. She had failed to produce another child. Her husband had grown dissatisfied with her and began beating her with the hope that she would divorce him which would, by Nuer law, ensure him an additional cow. Nyabieel told me this herself, and showed me the scars on her legs.

In America a year or so later, I had the last word of Nyabieel. It came on a piece of lined paper torn from a schoolboy's copy book and bore various messages to me, to which was added at the very end:

". . . and Jal, the one who is my brother-in-law, divorced his wife."

15

GOD ASKS FOR AN OX

The night was warm and friendly. The strong, somber glow of the full moon on the thatch-roofed huts and barns of the Nuer villagers made them look like the dwellings of gnomes and fairies. Pressed upon from above by the open sky, from a height marked by the farthest star, the little, peak-roofed buildings hugged the bare earth. They were indistinguishable, the one from the other, in either form or design, scarcely rising high enough above the ground to disturb the horizon, which ran in an unbroken circle around the rim of the earth. Out of the east flowed the river, level with its banks, shining like a curling silver ribbon, laid out and stuck upon the barren ground. The night was still, except for very simple noises: the barking of a dog, a baby crying, the sound of people singing. Soft and muffled sounds, they died quickly in this open, empty country of the south Sudan.

I had come up the river to Kuac's village, in the mission outboard, to attend a *pal,* which is a combination prayer service and sacrifice. I had been invited by an old woman whose name was Man Lul. She had once been a close companion to Kuac's mother, and as she grew older and less able to care for herself, Kuac asked me if I might not help her. I sometimes gave her money to buy grain; I also gave her old razor blades of my father's with which to cut her hair.

She lived alone. Her husband was dead. Her only son, Lul, by whose name she was known, for Man Lul means "the mother of Lul," had died when on a journey years before and had been buried by a stranger. Only recently the man had come to Man Lul asking for payment of one cow, which was due him according to the custom for burying her son. She had no cows and had come to me.

Man Lul had been baptized at the same time Kuac's older brother and sister were. She came to my Bible class in the dry season, announcing when the rains started that she would not be able to come now because the flooding river prevented her. She scarcely grasped the teaching of Christianity, but neither did she spurn it. Like many older people, she probably wondered what all the talk was about, for she believed in God, and it was not surprising that He would have a son. If He died for her, as the paper said, that was His business but it did not affect her very much. It happened a long time ago, and it was not pertinent to her life now. What was pertinent was how she was going to eat, and how she would get the cow to pay that man; and furthermore two relatives had been killed by lightning. This was much more pertinent, because it was something God had done *now*. It had happened in the village. They were in their hut. It burned, and they died. Why had they been singled out in this way? The paper did not answer this, but that was all right, the people know how to contact God. And they must, lest He continue to be angry with them and death come again. That was the purpose of the *pal* to which I had been invited.

I got out of the boat, pulled it out of the water, and was walking along in the direction of the singing. Cattle, tethered in front of the mud-walled barns, turned their heads to look at me. A dog ran out to the edge of the cattle and barked ferociously. Men and women, here and there, sat outside their huts, hunched over in a weary nighttime pose and watched me go by. Ahead was the hut and the enclosed yard where the people were singing. The sound of their voices ebbed and flowed in my ears. I stopped in the doorway of the cornstalk fence before going in. The moon, reflecting against my light cotton skirt and blouse and white skin, made me very obvious, but had much less effect upon the deep blue-black colored skin of the people sitting inside the yard on the ground.

I had never attended a *pal* before. I saw that the men and women sat in separate groups. In front of them, prancing back and forth along the fence, and waving a fly switch made of the end of a cow's tail attached to a short, wooden handle, was the song leader. He was draped in a long muslin cloth tied at one shoulder and he had a wide, two-inch ivory ring on his upper arm. His singing was irregular. The rhythm was quick, the melody haunting. The words were mumbled and difficult to follow. There was no end to the song. His voice rose above the others' at certain intervals in a solo, which began at a point high in the treble clef. Straining his voice he would pierce the night air, jabbing at it with a kind of screaming sound as he held aloft his fly switch, then descend the scale to a point where the rest would join in, in a lucid kind of chant.

I felt a strangeness about me, as if I did not belong. Yet I sensed I was among people who sought God, but the way they sought Him was alien and mysterious and incredible to me. If they were to convert me, I thought, what radical changes in my concepts of life would be necessary in order to adopt their frame of mind? How long would it take? And how would I look upon them if they did insist their way was right and mine was wrong? Would I call them fools? Impostors? Would I not tell them to let me alone?

The longer I stood in the doorway the more conspicuous I became. I walked into the yard, past the men and over to where the women were sitting, feeling very tall, very American, and very white. I sat down on the hard, bare ground near to Man Lul, covered my legs with my skirt to hide them from the mosquitoes, and felt the warm particles of sand and grit tickling my skin. The woman next to me stopped singing and moved her legs, which were stretched straight out in front of her. She said nothing to me, but kept slapping at the mosquitoes, which, by this time, had begun their insistent whining in my ears. I slapped at them too. Man Lul then reached her hand out in front of the woman and I shook it limply. I nodded to her in greeting and she smiled back, welcoming me. She was a tall woman, and very thin. Her head was small and angular. The hair on it was cropped close to the scalp. Part of the rim of her ear was missing, ripped off in a fight. Her cheeks were sunken, her lips only partially covered her one crooked front tooth, but her piercing eyes were alert with life. She reminded me of an ostrich—strangely ugly and very much a lady.

On the ground, facing us, was a woman in a bright red cotton dress, with her legs folded under her, sitting on the sole of one foot in the manner of women, with her hands loose in her lap. She was the prophetess of God. In the moonlight she appeared to be in a stupor with her head angled toward the ground. Above her the prancing, dancing song leader waved his fly switch around her head, bending over her, trying to waken her, but she did not respond.

The chanting never stopped. It would wax and then wane while children meandered about unconcernedly and babies slept on their mothers' laps. Overhead, Orion looked down on us, his sword hanging at his side. I listened intently, trying to hear the words of the song. Only certain ones were distinguishable to me. "Come, God, come. Good God. Great God. God of the whole earth." What is He supposed to do? I wondered. A dog came in. Men kept getting up to go out and urinate. Someone noticed the dog and clouted it with a stick. It yelped and left with its bony tail curved in a half-moon between its legs.

When an old man got to his feet and began to sing and dance, I asked the woman next to me why he was doing that.

"He is praying," she said, "the way you do in the house of God." It was a frustrating parallel, but hard to deny there in the moonlight, since what the man was doing was a far cry from what we did in the church; but to her, we were both calling on God.

The people had been singing, without pause, for perhaps an hour, and were noticeably tired. But the prophetess sat as dumb as stone, while the man kept up his singing and prancing, still waving his fly switch in the air. Near me an old woman sat dozing, with her head bobbing and her shoulder supporting a wooden pipe which reached from there to the ground. At the prolonged snapping of another woman's fingers she was aroused sufficiently to hand the pipe over to the next person who, discovering that it was out of charcoal, mumbled something down the line, and shortly a gourd was passed along containing a few hot coals.

It was getting darker now. The moon was moving away. Ahead of us a man called out disgustedly in an unabashed expression of Nuer arrogance, "What is the matter, God? We have been here a long time, now it is the middle of the night—why don't you come?" At this testimony of impatience, the song leader renewed his efforts and the people began to sing again with revived vigor. Soon, however, the leader's voice grew thin, and the people lapsed once more into their sleepy state, singing only halfheartedly, as they stared impassively at the woman in red, and waited for God to come.

Finally the song leader's efforts availed and the woman stirred. At this there was a new surge in the singing as the people anticipated God's response to their pleas. Straining his voice to the limit and concentrating on the woman, the leader sang wildly and waved the fly switch with quick, short jerks at her head, bending his agile body toward hers then backing away, again and again, slowly and deliberately. Lunging at her with his voice, he reached out for her, trying to tip her off balance and topple her from the realm of the physical into the mystic realm of spiritism.

The softness of her flesh was now frozen; the joints of every bone calcified. It was as though she were a statue, and the man was trying to make it speak. Suddenly, as if a light button had been flicked, her body began to snap and jerk sharply, as though she were being shocked with bolts of electricity. Now the singing had stopped, and the people were uttering many *ah*'s of relief and satisfaction.

The jerking became more violent and grotesque. With amazing strength, the woman hopped a rigid, heavy hop in quick succession across the ground on her folded legs. Straining to get to her feet, she unfolded herself and came to a standing position before the song leader who began immediately to prance around her, singing his piercing song and brandishing the floppy fly switch around her head.

The woman then set herself in motion, tilting her body slowly from side to side in her own dance, a weird, rhythmless affair, in which she had to drag herself about in front of us. Gradually her movements became more fluid, and as she danced, she sang, lifting her hands imploringly into the air, first one and then the other, giving the impression that she was pleading with God. She kept her head cocked at an angle, and from what I could see of her face in the moonlight, it was stern and unpleasant. After lumbering on for a time, she stopped abruptly and sat down.

The family was having this *pal*, Man Lul had told me, on the word of the sorceress who had said that God had killed the two men because certain cattle in the family had been used to buy a second wife for one man instead of their being used to marry a wife for a dead brother. Now the family was trying to make amends with God and pay for their mistake. This wild demonstration of the prophetess, which the people called "becoming drunk with God," indicated that God had now come to say what He wanted. It was down this avenue that peace came and whatever obedience God might demand through the woman, the people were ready to give. They knew now that they had gained His favor, proving to themselves again that their faith was well founded, and they waited with confidence.

The prophetess sat transfixed before us all, keeping us waiting for some time; then with a jerk of her head she motioned that she would speak. The men sitting right by her paid special attention, like executives about to hear the chairman of the board, but what she said was inaudible to the rest of us. We could only hear the men saying, "*Uh. Uh.*" Finally, in a voice we could all hear, she said that God did not like it because certain people were not in attendance. Where are they? He wanted to know. "They are coming," some people said. "They will be here tomorrow." And that was all at that time. The women began to get up. Man Lul and I got up and left the yard.

"Has sleep not killed you?" she said.

"*Uh,* sleep has killed me."

"Then let us go," she said. The granulated particles of hard clay crunched softly underfoot as we walked away. We passed by the huts now deserted. The people who had been sitting there earlier in the evening were gone. Only gray, muslin mosquito nets, like oblong tents, fluttered in the light breeze and marked where the people were. Outside the barns the cattle, tethered at their pegs, slept while the soft, white smoke from the dung fires rose over them, filling the air with its pungency, and drifted off across the river to the south, like a long, flowing scarf.

We did not go to Man Lul's hut where I had assumed I would spend the night, but we went to the hut of one of her relatives who had been at the *pal.* All I had with me was my washcloth and towel and blanket. She led me into the yard where, in the moonlight, I could see a woman and a man standing talking, and where at one side near the cornstalk fence and in a place by itself was a muslin mosquito net fixed above a low wooden bed. Man Lul left me standing just inside the fence and went over to where the others were. The woman with whom she spoke called out a name, and from under the mosquito net came a young girl who said to me, "Come. You will sleep here." I was surprised, expecting to sleep inside the hut with Man Lul, but it was obvious that the very best was being offered me, and I could not decline.

I ducked under the net, sat on the bed and pulled my legs in after me, then tucked the net in quickly. On the wobbly bed I spread out my blanket and lay down. The light of the moon came palely through the cloth. The hum of pursuing mosquitoes fell unheeded on my ear. The thin cotton mattress against my back felt comfortable, and soon I had fallen asleep.

The next morning, the heat of the sun coming through the cloth got me up. It was early, but the sky was as bright as midday. In the yard two chickens scratched at the dry earth picking up grain. Taking my towel and washcloth, I walked to the opening in the fence. Outside, a man sat against the cornstalks, bared to the sun, warming himself and pulling hairs out of his chin. I followed the footpath across an open space, and along the high grass next to the water's edge. The river was narrow up to the bend, then it broadened and looked like a small lake level with the land.

Pulled into the reeds along the path was a dugout canoe with a lot of water in it to keep it from drying out and cracking. It had not been a very straight tree trunk, and now it sat at an angle in the water. Half of its side had been mudded over where the wood had rotted away, leaving big holes. I took off my shoes and got in and walked to the back where I stood, steadying myself as the current played with the canoe. I unwrapped my towel and took out the toothpaste tube and my toothbrush and put them down on the flat surface at the rear where the paddler sat next to the water, and threw the towel over my shoulder. Taking off my glasses, I hung them over the side of the dugout, then dipped my hand into the stream and brought the cool water to my face and dried it with the towel. Then I took my toothbrush and held the handle between my teeth while I unscrewed the top of the tube and squeezed the toothpaste out. Having brushed my teeth over the side of the dugout and washed my mouth in the muddy water, I got out, dried my feet, and put on my shoes.

It was still early and there was no one about. No children dogged my steps as they would be doing if they had known I was there, so I walked on upstream. I was alone. I liked being alone, and I was happy. Around the bend of the river, where the river widens, I came upon a spoonbill stork standing in a shallow place behind a screening of river grass, fishing, swishing his long flat bill from side to side under the surface of the water. Spoonbills usually travel in pairs, I had read, which had proved to be true at another time and in another place, where I had first seen spoonbills, a pair, feeding in a sandy place following a tropical downpour, in ankle deep water. I had watched them from my veranda through binoculars.

This one was alone. I stood motionless. He stepped slowly and precisely through the water, swishing his bill back and forth, quickly and smoothly, his graceful white neck dipped low. Then somehow

he knew it—he knew I was there, and lifted his head, standing tense on thin, brittle-looking legs, holding his neck and body high. His flat, wet, black bill glistened, his white feathers shone, his round eye stared at me. Alerted to danger, he hunched his shoulders, spread his wings, and was off—black legs trailing, upstream, across the river, across the swamp, until his white feathers blended with the faded blue of the sky and I could see him no more.

I had been gone from the village long enough, and if Man Lul had come looking for me she would wonder where I was, so I turned and headed back the way I had come. On my right were the tawny-looking huts and barns of the villagers on the gray-colored plain, and on my left, the river and the swamp. A black-and-white kingfisher flew up from his perch on the side of the dugout as I passed, hovered above the river with his wings beating the air and his head bent downward, his sharp beak a poised spear. Then he dived, letting himself fall at great speed and hit the water. There was a splash and he was up again and back to the side of the dugout, a small fish clamped sideways in his long thin bill. It's the river, I thought, that makes living on the plain bearable. It's the river and the birds it brings; its the movement of the river—it comes from someplace and goes someplace and makes you feel that you can go too, if you want to or have to.

Ahead, in the straight of the river, before it turned again and went out of sight around another bend, a canoe came slowly along the side, a few inches out from the reeds. In it a man stood fishing, while another man paddled at the back. I could see him throw his spear and reach for it again. It was not baited or hooked; it was pointed and barbed. If he caught any fish it was mostly luck. He might notice a certain swaying or parting of the reeds and throw his spear into the muddy water, but he could not see the fish. He was fishing for *ruel*, a smooth fish, like trout, only much bigger with beady eyes and a thin, pointed face, and could weigh fifteen pounds or more. It was good eating fried in deep fat and coated with an egg batter. It was not as good as Nile perch though. Nothing was as good as that.

I did not pass through the village to get back to the place where I had stayed the night. That place faced the river and I walked up to the entrance in the fence and went in. The sun was up higher now, filling the whole yard with light. The girl who had got out of the bed the night before was pounding grain with a pole in a mortar made in the earth. The pole was worn smooth and clean where she held it with the fingers of her hands spread wide apart. Her toes were humped as they dug the ground, braking the movement and giving her balance. She lifted the pole high above her head and brought it down with a thud into the earth mortar. Round kernels of grain ran up the side and fell back again. Up and down, up and down the pole went. Thud . . . thud . . . thud. For some reason the sight and the sound reminded me of the old oil well beside our schoolhouse when I was a child, which beat out a slow dull rhythm all day long. I used to watch the long wooden beam rise and fall as the wheel went around from my desk by the window.

The bed had been stripped, the mattress and the mosquito net were gone. I sat down on the rawhide webbing and watched the girl as I waited for Man Lul. I wondered when the *pal* would reconvene—I didn't want to miss any part of it. I thought of asking the girl, but I did not. She would say, "In a little while" or "I don't know." It did not matter to her when it started; it did not matter to anybody. It *would* start, they all knew that. That was what mattered.

A small boy came through the doorway, followed by a dog with its ears cut short. The boy stopped when he saw me and stared. He was still standing there, with his hands clasped behind his head, a long-legged little creature, in a gray suit not made with cloth but from the fine dung ash in which he had slept the night, when Man Lul appeared and came over to me.

"Is it good peace?" she said.

"It is good peace, old mother," I said.

She was wearing just the *pac,* which all women wore, a kind of skirt which dropped from her hips halfway to her knees, gaping open at the side where the tie ends came together and were tucked in at the top to secure the cloth.

"Has hunger not killed you?" she said.

"No, not yet," I said.

She was looking straight at me, smiling faintly as the corner of her mouth quivered characteristically.

"Have the people come together?" I said.

"No, they have not yet come," she said. "Will you not eat now?"

"It is good," I said. "I will eat."

"*Uh*, let us go."

As we went out of the yard I took my camera off the fence where I had put it the night before and walked behind her. The sun was hot now. The flies were out and sticking to my face and back. We crossed the open stretch of ground to her hut, which sat off by itself, and went into the yard. It was a new hut with fresh yellow thatch perched squarely on the mud wall, not slouching to one side as old roofs did.

"This is my house," she said proudly. "I just finished it in these days." The quiver at the corner of her mouth was back again, her crooked tooth shone in the sun. "I did it, I by myself. It was a big work."

"I know it," I said. "Did you cut the thatching grass, too?"

"*Uh*," she said with a special emphasis, "look at my hands." She spread open her palms in front of me, and I saw and felt how rough they were.

On either side of the hut was a grain platform. The legs of each platform were made of cornstalks tied together in bunches, with sticks across the top of the cornstalk framework holding the drying heads of grain. A green tobacco plant was still growing beside the hut, under the thatch, and behind it were two large clay pots upturned. I tried to imagine this as my home—this little round enclosure of sticks and mud covered with thatch. Would this dark little room give me security under this vast expanse of empty sky and plain? And I tried to imagine my mother coming out of this hut on her hands and knees, going to get supper or to get water at the river. But I could not do it, no more, I suppose, than Man Lul could imagine living in my house with its four, square, unfriendly walls and cold interior; nor than she could imagine cooking on a stove or turning a faucet to get her water.

"Come," Man Lul said and led me over to a cornstalk enclosure she had made in the fence. "Sit down," she added, pointing to her sleeping skin she had put there on the ground for me to sit on. As I sat down, she left and then returned with a large bowl-shaped gourd full of dura porridge, which she had made from her own grain. She set it down in front of me with another gourd of a different shape, more like a fat wine bottle, which had milk in it. "This is sweet milk," she said. "Eat." Then she left. A woman never eats with a guest.

I took the twisted leather cap off the top of the long-necked gourd and poured the milk out onto the porridge. Then I took the aluminum serving spoon, which was standing straight up in the middle of the porridge, and mixed the two together. I had learned to do it this way. My first experience, some years before, had baffled me and the people had laughed. Don't you know how to eat, Nyarial? they said. At that time, a man picked up the milk gourd and upset it into the porridge, and it came gurgling out in thick curds. Then he stirred the milk into the porridge with a shell spoon, scraping around the sides of the gourd as one scrapes the batter in a mixing bowl. "Eat," he said, and sat back to watch me.

The sweet milk was especially for me. My grandmother loved buttermilk, but I never did. I was glad I could tell the people about my grandmother. I felt it left me less queer in their eyes if I could assure them that one of my relatives agreed with them, if I could not. For they loved sour milk. It was good that they did. Keeping milk sweet in that country was a problem. They never tried. Instead, they sometimes flavored the sour milk by adding steer urine to it. I had never discussed milk with Man Lul, that I could remember, but it was typical that any salient fact about me would be common knowledge to everyone.

It was pleasant eating her food. Everything was lovely and clean. The milk I knew was not hers, for she had no cow. Someone had given it to her for me. When Man Lul returned she looked at the gourd, which was still one third full.

"Nyarial, why do you not eat?" she said.

"My stomach is full, old mother," I said.

"*Uh,* you have no stomach," she said. I laughed. This was as good a defense as any so I left it that way and said, "It is very good porridge, old mother. It is very smooth."

"What kind of a woman would I be," she said, "if the porridge was lumpy?"

"It would not be good," I said.

She took the gourds away. She would finish the porridge herself later. I went outside the hut and waited for Man Lul.

She came out wearing a purple-dyed muslin cloth over her short skirt. Going over to the grain platform, she reached a pair of sneakers off the top. I recognized them. They had been mine.

"Look, my daughter," she said, showing them to me, "they are old, what will I do?" She studied them for a moment.

"I do not know, old mother," I said. "They are truly old." At the front of the shoes the cloth had separated from the rubber soles, and the backs of each of them were tramped down, even with the heel. Each shoe was tied around with string as reinforcement.

"Look at these, my feet," she said, turning her foot around so that I could see the heel. "It is very sore, my daughter. Look, don't you see? It is split. The skin has dried."

"*Uh,* I see it truly, old mother," I said. "When the rain comes it will soften again." She put the sneakers down and slid her feet into them; then we went out of the yard, she ahead of me.

Man Lul's life consisted of her grain field and her goat, when she had one. The field she hoed and planted herself, then harvested the grain. She was a kind of African dowager, proud of her heritage, jealous of her privacy, grounded in her dignity, beholden to no one.

"Where is your field, old mother?" I asked as we walked across the empty space toward the village.

She stopped and turned around. "There," she said, pointing with an outstretched arm to a place behind her hut. I could see the flat, black, stubbly plain going off in all directions. "It is across there. One side has the anthill—over there." She raised her voice to show the far length of it. The anthill I could see. "The other side has grass."

I could see some brown grass standing in a patch by itself. Between the anthill and the grass was quite a large area. "My field and the field of Man Guek are together," she said, then looked me straight in the eye and held her gaze as if to say, What do you think of it, and of me for being as old as I am and still hoeing my own field?

"All of that is yours?" I said. "It is a big one, truly. It is big work for you, I think." She bowed her head a trifle and chuckled.

"I do it, I myself," she said, and I thought of her on her hands and knees, in the muddy soil, hoeing the grain. She did not begin to move, still concentrating on our conversation, preparing to say something else.

"The boys," she said, then stopped as if to let it sink in, "they have a bad way. They play for no reason and do not watch the sheep. When the sheep came into my field, my heart burned, truly. I said to them, 'You boys, if it is repeated, I will take you before the chief.' " She was plainly disgruntled. I felt that I should be too, for her sake, but she turned away, and began walking in the direction of the *pal,* where the singing had begun again.

The sun was halfway to the zenith. Its white light covered the sky, bleaching out the faded blue until it seemed the sky was gone altogether. The cattle were being set free and followed out to pasture. Oxen lowed and tossed their heads. Cowbells tinkled. Under the oxen's creaking hooves the earth was pulverized, the dust was stirred and picked up by the breeze and carried into the atmosphere where it would stay for six months, reflecting the heat, clouding the sun, until the rains came again.

"The people are happy," Man Lul said, as we drew near.

"Why?" I inquired.

"Because the ox was drunk. Last night, they say, the ox was drunk. It is the happiness of God, they say."

She spoke of the sacrificial ox, but I did not know how you could tell an ox had become drunk.

We came to the place and went into the yard. Man Lul went over and sat right down with the women. I sat in back of her. People were still standing about, but the prophetess was in her place, sitting on a grass mat that I could now see in the daylight. In front of her were two calabashes filled with water. She had on her red dress and was sitting as she had the night before with her hands in her lap, feet folded under her, her head at an angle, looking numb. The song leader was working on her, waving his fly switch madly at her head as he sang his frantic song.

I noticed that something new had been put up in the yard next to the woman. I leaned over, "Old mother," I said, "that *yik,* it has just been brought?"

"*Uh,*" she answered turning her head sideways.

"Whose talk was that?"

"It was the talk of God," she said. "The prophetess said so."

I looked at the shorn sapling stuck in the ground. It had just been cut, the bark was still green. There was a *yik* in every yard. It marked the place where the bones of the sacrifice were put. It was the closest approximation to the Old Testament idea of an altar that the culture had. We had used the word *yik* in the translation of Genesis and Exodus. However, in the book of Exodus God made very clear the type of altar He wanted, explaining in detail how it should be made. Given the advantage of knowing that the Old Testament account was truly the Word of God, one had no problem deciding that the Nuer *yik* was false. But from the people's point of view, who is to say which talk is true, the talk of the prophetess, or the talk of the paper? If it only could be established once and for all that the talk of the paper is the true talk of God, then it would be simply a matter of hearing it from cover to cover to discover that the *yik* is outmoded, and that another plan has taken its place. Unfortunately, this was not an easy point to get across. We were at an impasse from the start.

Perspiration stood out in heavy beads on the song leader's face and began running down his cheeks and the back of his neck. The singing was in full volume now, but the woman remained limp and unresponsive. Although the strangeness of the night before seemed less pronounced, and I felt more oriented to what was going on—though disappointed in the quality of the "magic"—nevertheless, I was conscious of the faith being exercised by those about me. The Bible says, "Faith is the substance of things hoped for, the evidence of things unseen." Here the people were hoping for God to lift His wrath. I could not deny that there was more earnestness in these worshipers than one found in Christian churches at home. There was more at stake. Theologically, of course, they were thousands of years behind.

The prophetess continued to drag out her part of the program by maintaining her otherworldly attitude while the people sang. I could not help but wonder how she had spent the night, whether she had yawned or cracked a smile, or slapped at mosquitoes. From the group in front of her, a young man got on his knees and began crawling up to where she sat. Before approaching her, he dipped some water out of one of the gourds with a smaller gourd next to it, and handed it to her. Confidently he bowed his head as she poured water out upon his legs, then stroked them firmly with her hands. I presumed the boy was suffering from yaws, which would make his bones ache.

When he went away, an old man took his place. He threw back his gray-colored cloth as if in pantomime, and placed his thumb at the hip joint of his long lean thigh, pressed it hard against the bone, signifying the place of his pain, while he supported himself on the palm of one hand. The woman studied him momentarily, then touched the spot with her finger which satisfied the man, and he crawled solemnly away. Ah, I thought, so this is why my touch is so profitable to an ailing body. We white people are as prophets to the people, with spiritual power to heal the sick. Because we associate ourselves with God, they therefore expect the kind of cures familiar to them.

Now a woman got up and walked forward. She was Man Guek, Man Lul's friend. They had been baptized together, and her son, a schoolteacher, was a friend of Kuac's. She took off a metal bracelet and put it on the arm of the prophetess. Then she kissed the bracelet. People kissed whomever they venerated. Old women kissed the doctor's feet. Doctors and prophets were similar. They had control of people's bodies. They both called on God.

The impassive prophetess sat enshrouded in her atmosphere of hocus-pocus. The song leader sang lustily on. With no further prompting, and in what seemed to be her own good time, she got to her feet in the slow-motion technique of the night before, and eased herself into the same drunken dance step. As she danced she sang, not in the low chant of the people, but wildly, imitating the song leader.

She inspired confidence in everyone but me. She was able to give vent to her feelings from within the thin veil enveloping her, separating her from the rest of us. I was not certain what was causing this phenomenon of the human spirit. I wanted to break in and ask her to explain herself. I did not mind crediting the devil with this production if he were responsible for it, but I was reluctant to give him more credit than was his due. I tended to think that the woman had quite a bit of personal talent for this kind of thing. That her success depended upon audience participation and approval disqualified her from being great.

I thought carefully of the mesmerization of minds which occurs in Christendom. I, too, had participated in services where God was being called upon to "speak to hearts." I had experienced the subtleties of audience manipulation designed to elicit response. At the end of an evangelistic service, I thought, why must "the organ play softly, *Is Your All on the Altar,*" while "everyone's head is bowed," and "Christians are praying"?

Or, what makes legitimate the act of lighting tapers in a darkened sanctuary, at a central candle symbolizing Jesus Christ the Light of the World, which young people take in their hands in an act of dedication and sing "I'll Go Where you Want Me to Go, Dear Lord"?

Who *are* the true worshipers of God, I wondered. Jesus said, ". . . those who are real worshipers will worship the Father in spirit and in truth. Such are the worshipers whom the Father wants." It is not because we worship under a certain auspices within the Christian framework which guarantees our worship. Have we not all made up our rituals? Had not even the Jews?

The song leader strained at his voice and waved the fly switch in close proximity to the dancing woman, as though he were accompanying her. Presently she wearied and brought herself to a halt in a standing position in front of the people, with her hands hanging at her sides. Sullenly she demanded our attention. She had no competitors, and her awesome attitude seemed overplayed to an audience which had been waiting since the night before to hear her speak.

Ignoring the prejudices already formed in my mind, I tried to assume the role of a novice about to experience a new thing, but my attention was broken by the woman's ludicrous appearance. The red cotton dress hung unevenly above her knees. The armholes gripped at her arms; the waistline was around her chest. Under the dress was a skirt which formed a lower border. The sun had so warmed the woman's body that the perspiration on her face and forehead reflected the light in various places, accentuating her humanity. But as if convinced of her divinity, she looked us over, moving her eyes very slowly from one side to the other, then began to speak in a quiet, faraway tone of voice.

"You all know," she said, "that I am not the person of a little while ago speaking to you, do you not?"

"*Uh,*" the people chorused.

"You know that I am God speaking to you, do you not?"

"*Uh,*" the people said again. At this point I was lost in a moment of incredulity comparable to a time in Rome when, with a group of tourists in St. Peter's Cathedral, a woman guide drew our attention to a lighted glass crypt containing some bones in disarray, which, she said, belonged to, indeed *were,* St. Peter's bones. Now, as then, I wanted proof. But proof is the desire of the skeptic and is unnecessary to believers.

I was unable to hear all the prophetess said, for she did not speak for everyone to hear, but the gist of her message was that God now wanted the ox. The people gave their assent and the woman sat down. Normal commotion followed as men got up and went out, and those who were left passed several wooden pipes back and forth to smoke. After a length of time, calculated by no one but me, noise outside the fence gave the advanced notice of the arrival of the ox.

It entered, an ashen-gray beast with a large set of lyrelike horns crowning its oblong head. If God were the least bit particular, I thought upon seeing it, He would not be pleased with this offering. It was a picture of total resignation, weighed down, one might muse, with the human burden for which it was responsible. But what was more obviously the case, it was resigned to die because of illness, and the people were making profitable use of it before death came.

The graceful horns were the only beautiful feature left of what must once have been a proud, ponderous, gentlemanly ox. Now they seemed too much for him to carry, and his head drooped pitifully. He stood docilely by, oblivious to all that was taking place. There was no light in his eye; no power in his legs. His tail hung down, inert like a slack rope. No one wholly feared his strength. If someone could have said to him, "Die," I think he would have, gladly.

By now the people were on their feet. I sensed a tremor of excitement among them. The ox, acting somewhat bewildered, locked his legs and refused to go. Only a braided grass rope around his neck held him captive. Three men attended him, clucking reassuringly in the language all cattle understood. The animal began to move slowly into the middle of the yard where there was a tethering peg, freshly hewn and stripped of its bark for the occasion. To it the animal was tied, and against it, it pulled, backing around in a taut circle, its hooves creaking and digging up the earth. Kindly, almost tenderly, the men handled it as if in sympathy for its inevitable end. They stroked the dusty gray neck, and patted firmly the bony rump, one man keeping a hand on its tail.

The people were themselves in readiness to run if the animal should suddenly bolt. Even the prophetess was wary and kept moving back and forth with the others. I raised my camera to take a picture and when I put it down saw that she was concerned, and was making signs to me with her face. I thought I may have affected her sense of the rightness of things by using my camera, and had decided I should have to be more careful with the next picture, when a few of the people spoke to me and told me that the prophetess was afraid I might get hurt.

It interested me that she should be concerned for my safety, and I wondered if some of her humanity had not slipped past the veil, and that she was being to me what she would otherwise be, outside the trance. I went on to wonder whether she was wondering who I thought she was, and whether she spoke to me as God, or not.

I moved back with the rest to watch the men who were still humoring the ox. It was by no means an anonymous animal. It belonged. Its name was known by everyone there. It was a part of history; without it and its kind the *family* would have been anonymous, such was the import of cattle in the Nuer way of life.

After the ox had quieted down, two men went to its head, and another, an older man with a thick ivory bracelet on his arm, came up to them carrying a calabash of water. The men lifted the animal's head, forcing open its mouth while the old man poured in the water in an act of purification. The ox tried to back out of the men's hands, and again the spectators were on the alert, but the excitement was of no consequence. Then the prophetess emerged from the group holding a spear in her right hand, and took a few steps forward to the broadside of the ox. There, her otherworldly attitude gave way to genuine feminine timidity before the beast. She held the spear as one might if he were expecting to drop it quickly and run, and made a feeble, halfhearted thrust into the animal's side. The people stepped back against the fence, but the ox only turned its head and looked back at the woman with dull, forlorn eyes.

The spear blade had nicked the skin, and the prophetess had presumably initiated the death process. She handed the spear to the man at the animal's rump, who clenched the shaft in his fist close to the spearhead and jabbed it into the ox's side. The head of the ox dropped low, but the animal did not fall. He jabbed four more times before it finally reeled and fell with a thud, its feet sticking into the air, then rolling back to the ground.

It had not protested or made a sound against its executioners. Now it lay prostrate and leaden-eyed, its tail flung out behind, its blood splattered bright red on the ground. He had fallen on the right side, which was further evidence of God's approval.

The people standing about eyed the body of the ox greedily. It would be divided among them with the choicest parts going to those with highest priority. The stomach and the hump were two of the choicer parts. The head would be cooked and the meat eaten, and the skull-bone would be placed at the base of the sapling in the yard. The carcass would be hacked to pieces there on the ground, and the portions handed out on the spot. There would be shoutings, arguing, and threatenings as disappointed, less eligible persons received the undesirable parts.

The women were busy bringing out the clay pots of beer when I walked over to Man Lul to tell her I was leaving. She was sitting with some of the women, talking and smoking an old pipe. "You are going?" she repeated my statement as a question.

"*Uh,*" I said.

She got up unaided and with breath to spare. We walked out of the yard, she ahead of me. The sun was overhead.

"Was it good?" she asked after we had left the yard and I was bidding her goodbye. She had turned her head toward me and was looking again into my face. She belonged to the twentieth century, albeit disguised in the primitivism of the Nuer people, this old woman, tall and straight, without an ounce of flabby flesh anywhere on her body.

I respected her and the pride of her people and was hesitant to speak. Of course, she did not mean to be asking a hard question. She meant, did I appreciate the ways of her people? Did I enjoy myself? Was my curiosity satisfied?

"Yes, it was good, old mother," I said. "But I have a doubt in my heart. My doubt is the death. The death of the ox. This, too, is bad. Death has no good in it." Then we parted.

I could have said to her, Jesus died for our sins. He did away with cattle sacrifice. God does not want our sacrifices; they don't do any good. But she had heard that many times. It was not a question of "giving her the Gospel." It was the problem of making her understand.

The boat slid easily into the water and floated backward into the stream. Teal rose in a flurry from their hiding place in the reeds and fluttered off in a wobbly line, whistling as they flew. I started the motor and turned the boat downstream. The boat rose on the step and skimmed over the river. The force of the wind in my face cheered me. The sight of the wide, sweeping plain lifted my soul. But the gulf between me and the people seemed wider than it had ever been. How, I thought, are they to discern the distinction between the sacrifice of men for God, and the sacrifice of God for men?

16

THE SKY CANOE

There was an old man named Yuol whose life encouraged us. He had been ill for some years with tuberculosis, the great enemy of the Nuer people. A relative who had had the same disease and had been treated successfully at the mission came to Yuol one day with a Gospel of John and asked if he would like to have it read to him. Yuol said Yes, and listened intently to the reading. He liked what he heard. He said it was good talk. He asked to hear the words again. The more he heard them the more he liked them. He told his relative it was good talk every time he heard them.

The young man said, "You must go to the place of magic and get injected. You will get better there as I did." The old man had never been to the mission before, but he came, and was given a hut in the line of huts for the in-patients, where he stayed for treatment for many months.

Yuol's skin was black as the soil underfoot. He had large, wrinkled hands, a wide, happy face, and kept his gray hair shaved close. Sometimes he wore a white cloth, sometimes only the wide ivory arm-bracelets of his tribe. All during his treatment he listened whenever someone talked the talk of God. At the clinic prayer time he listened. At the church he listened. And at the weekly Bible study he listened. I first knew him there. He was delighted with the talk of God. It made him laugh at himself. How many cows have I killed for the gods? he would say. One, two, three, four, five—he counted them out on the fingers of both hands for everyone to see. And did I get life?

No, no life, he would answer himself in front of us. They are gods of uselessness.

During the time I knew him, which was not more than two years, he would say things to indicate what the Holy Spirit might say to a man. "Nyarial," he said, "do you know what God wants of us? He wants us to be praisers."

Another time he said, "You know, Nyarial, if the house of the white people is so big and fine, what will the house of God in the sky be like?"

"And Nyarial," he said once, "come, I must tell you something. I think I know why Jesus wasn't afraid to die. Do you know? Because He knew His Father would take care of Him. Do you think that is right, Nyarial?"

Serious, thoughtful, seeking, the old man never tired of talking about "Jeebeth," as he called Jesus.

I was standing in the kitchen beating an egg one day. "Nyarial!" I heard my name. The old man had come into the house and was standing behind me, but I had neither heard nor seen him come. I was going away and he knew it, and I said to him, *"Ah,* old father, what is it?"

"Nyarial," he said, "what will I do when you go? Who will talk with me?" I looked at him in surprise. His smile was gone now. I did not realize he was serious, but now I could see he was.

"I think God will send someone," I said. "I don't know who it will be," I added, unwilling to disappoint him, and not knowing whether I had any right to involve God in his dilemma or not.

He went out and I kept on with my work.

Soon he was back. "Nyarial! Nyarial!" he called to me from the veranda. "Koang has come. Koang has come. Nyarial, come here, Koang has come!"

I went out to see and Yuol, coming in the doorway, took both my hands and led me out and down the path to Koang who was coming toward me, a tall old man with a faded blanket around his shoulders, walking with a long cane. He had been a big chief during the British rule of the country, and he had a large family, many wives and a big name, but he had had much sorrow, too, and had lost some of his sons in the prime of their youth. He had come to the clinic as a cataract patient, hardly able to see, and there he had met Yuol who befriended him. Together they would sit outside their hut and talk and talk, Yuol and Koang, in the heat, in the sun, about Jesus. Koang listened, and began to hear and eventually he, too, began to laugh and to count the cattle he had sacrificed to *Lual* and *Deng* and *Wiu* and the other gods. "Did we find life?" Yuol had asked his friend. "Did the cows bring us life?" And both men knew that the cows had not always brought them what they wanted.

Now Koang had returned unexpectedly, after having gone back to his village for a time. His coming had made old Yuol glad, so that he said to me, "Now you can go, my daughter, for Koang has come, God has brought him."

You never knew what Yuol might say. "I sleep beside the father of evil," he had said one day.

"Who is that?"

"My wife. She will not hear the talk of God. She fights with the other woman." (The other woman was his younger wife.)

"I called to that man, Ruon, one day," he said. "I said, 'Come, let us talk.' He came. I said, 'You are an old man. Let us talk about the God, Jesus.' He said, 'I don't want to talk about Jesus.' I said, 'Go away. I don't have any other talk.' "

One day as I was going along the river path I saw him back by the clinic huts with his hand in the air, beckoning me—not to come, but to listen: "It is sweet. It is sweet. It is sweet," he was saying.

I raised my hand in the air to answer. "It is so. It is so. It is so," I said.

When his treatment was finished he was told that he could go home. He was much stronger now, and he rose early in the morning, eager for the journey in the dugout canoe which would be followed by seven days of walking before he reached his village. I went to his hut to say goodbye to him, and found him happy because he was going home. But that was not all. Yuol was going home believing that Jesus Christ was God.

He prayed that morning, "God of the sky, Father of Jesus, protect me from the father of evil when I get home. You know the temptations and the power of our customs. O, protect me."

The last words I heard that morning watching him drift away in the loaded dugout were, "He is my husband! God is my husband!" This was to him a reality, for he had no questionings in his heart that day concerning the nearness or the love of God for him.

We who remained at the mission heard reports of how the old man reached his village, and how he carried out his desire to tell his family of the talk of God by calling them together to speak and to pray with them. It was early in December that the word reached us of his weakened condition. "He won't live long," the messenger said; "he can never reach Kuanylualthoaan by foot again. He is dying. The disease of before has come again."

But that was not all the message. We listened eagerly as the man went on to say that Yuol had sacrificed an ox to please the family. A son had died. He himself was dying. That was all the family needed. "Appease God and live, or let us live," was their pressured plea. It was too much for him. Utterly alone in his faith, he succumbed to their incessant pleadings and threats and the animal was killed.

He was to us like a brother in trouble, and our first thought was to go to him as quickly as possible. The Devil was not going to beguile this lone sheep of the Lord's in this way without some opposition. Had he not "laid a snare for our feet" many times and had not one of God's own children comforted and encouraged us until our hearts were renewed? This we must do for Yuol.

The only way to travel quickly was to go by the Missionary Aviation Fellowship plane. This we did, landing at the mission station closest to Yuol's village. From there we set out by Jeep down the government dirt road to Yuol's village where we learned that he was not there, but had gone to the cattle camp. We then found a young man who knew the country, and he led us across the trackless plain, through the tall grass and over the hummocked terrain. There were no villages to mark the way, only a tree in the distance, standing like a black mast on a calm, golden sea of grass. "Go there," the boy said, "go to that tree." So we went forward, through the wall of grass, creeping over the hummocks in four-wheel drive, lurching back and forth on the springless seats.

There was nothing at that tree and the boy repeated, "Go there," pointing with his arm stretched out like a saber across to the horizon, a distance marked by nothing at all but the endlessness of the lifeless yellow grass.

Finally, as we persisted in pushing back the blank horizon, the boy said, "He is there." We looked and at first saw nothing, but as our vision narrowed to the point in the distance at the tip of his stretched-out fingers, we saw another tree very small, and thin and lifeless against the dull gray sky. It was there that we finally found him, by a waterhole, camped with the young men and the cattle. As the Jeep came closer to the tree, he saw us and came out to meet us, walking through the grass, leaning on a staff, his old body bent, but draped in the white cloth we had given him, his head bared to the blazing sun.

We ran up to him and greeted him, and he clasped our hands, saying, "My children, I am dying. I am dying," briefing us immediately on the one thing that mattered.

We walked back to the tree and he sat down within the parallel lines of its lone shadow and told us his story. "My son died, and I am dying," he said. "There has been much trouble."

Reet sat there with us. An older man himself who had known trouble, he had worked in the clinic and had known Yuol. He was a believer and had known the testings which evolve in the face of tribal custom. He listened and was not surprised; nor was he dissuaded in the patience and love of God for men. "I did something," Yuol went on. "I killed an ox. The father of evil came. My head was confused. The people were angry. They said God was angry and it was my fault—that was why we were dying."

In spite of all his trouble he was not bitter with God, and after admitting to his own failure he then began to speak of Jesus. We all joined him in this, speaking that name as the oasis each one of us knew Him to be. There was relief and joy and the knowledge of the love of God. It was as unmistakable as the heat of the sun burning down on us.

"We have come to take you back with us, old father," we said.

"*Ah,* the journey would kill me," he said.

"But there is the sky canoe which is coming to take you back tomorrow."

He held his head in his hands, thinking, and then finally he agreed to go.

It is amazing that the arduous trip back, through the grass, over the hummocks, lurching with each twist of the wheel did not kill him. But Reet held him in the seat, supporting him with his arm, trying to cushion the blows.

After an hour's crawl through the grass, the Jeep came out to the dirt road at a lone merchant's shop. When the Arabs there saw us they looked surprised.

"Who are those two white women?" they said.

"They came to get the old man, the one there in the car."

"Who is he?" the one Arab said.

"He's that old man from Pi Jiaak," the other Arab explained, "the one who is a person of Jesus."

What a reputation, I thought; even the Arabs know who he is and what he thinks. If they know, everyone must know.

The next day we flew back to the mission. Yuol lived one month—and on the day marking the first anniversary of his baptism, he died. The day before he died I had gone to see him, and had sat beside him where he lay on the floor of the hut. He had had a stroke which paralyzed his right side. His speech was affected and his strength was almost gone. But he recognized me and said my name, then he fumbled around to find my hand which he held while he tried to speak, so determined was he to tell me something. I bent down to hear him better as he labored over every word.

He said, "My daughter, I am dying. Do not bury me in the way of the people. Cover me only with the white cloth of the girls.

Nothing else." He meant not to bury him with heathen ritual, using his sleeping skin as a covering, but to use the cloth we had given him instead. He began to cough violently. His chest heaved up and down. I thought he was choking. Finally he stopped and I told him, "Yes, old father, you will be buried in the white cloth as you said," and his face relaxed, and he closed his eyes.

The next morning was when he died. I went back to see him early, but he never spoke again. Only his eyes moved back and forth where he lay on his sleeping skin, on the floor, as he breathed heavily and irregularly. I do not know if he recognized me or not.

An old woman sat in the hut, just inside the door, sucking at her pipe and keeping her eye on Yuol. She was a patient herself, but not related to Yuol, which meant that she was immune to the death at work in him and free from the fear of it. The sunlight coming through the doorway fell across her legs and stopped short of the center of the hut floor. It was cool inside, but outside, the clay yard, the hut opposite us, and the back side of the brick clinic at the end of the path were colorless in the sun's glare.

Presently the woman said, "He will die today?" She thought I really knew, because I was a white person and a person of God, as the people called us.

"I don't know," I said, looking over at her, "maybe he will, his body has nothing more." She looked very intent but it was because she was working so hard with her pipe. "Did Yuol talk to you of the God, Jesus?" I said.

"*Uh,*" she said.

"And did he tell you about the place he is going to when he dies?"

"*Uh,* he said he was going to the place where God is."

"Which God?"

"The God, Jesus."

"Do you believe this is true?"

She lifted her eyes looking up at me while she sucked away on her pipe. It wasn't burning well. And I didn't expect her to answer me. The people believed that when a person dies he ceases to be "person" and becomes "spirit" or ghost. He has a spirit body and appears to people at night in dreams. He can see and speak, but he does not hear—at least there is no exchange of conversation with him. Spirits are usually men, although a woman who is badly treated on the earth sometimes appears as a woman spirit. If this happens the family takes a goat and a black earthen pot, kills the goat, and sticks its head in the pot and so buries it. This is to mean that the woman spirit will return no more.

However, if a man spirit appears and demands a wife, because he was overlooked and a living male relative took a wife first, the family will have a sacrifice and give the living man's new wife to the dead man. (Because of the custom that dead men marry he can make such a demand.)

Spirits have their own villages and cattle which have been sacrificed to them, but they do nothing with these cattle. The people say that when a person dies he does not know the path to *kuoth caka*—the God of creation.

I waited to see if the woman was going to answer my question, but she had to fix her pipe first. Finally she said, "I don't know" just at the moment Yuol seemed to stop breathing, which she noticed immediately and added, "He died?"

"No," I said, "he is breathing still." But, I thought, it won't be long—and why is it that of the three of us, it is you, old woman, who does not understand? Are you doomed, old woman, because you cannot understand?

"The place of God is a good place, old mother," I said. "Maybe there is cattle there."

"It is like that?" she said.

"It may be. God said He was getting it ready for us." Little did I know if there were cattle in heaven, but whatever there would be, would be good, and to the Nuer nothing was as good as cattle. I was actually excited because this was the first and only person I had ever seen die in hope, and I had seen many people die. I wanted someone to share this with.

There were long lapses in the old man's breathing. The woman was aware of it, as was I. "He dies," she said, then shot a stream of saliva out the door. We sat in silence for a long time. I kept watching Yuol, never looking away from him, trying to imagine the journey he was making "through the valley of the shadow of death," and it was as though I were walking with him, knowing that soon we would have to part.

I was thinking, too, of the rest of the psalm, "I will fear no evil, for Thou art with me" and my mind boggled at what Yuol must be knowing now, and at what he would come to know—that whereas on earth he had been of most men primitive, soon he would know something that no man on earth could know, and I concentrated on the revelation which awaited this simple, humble man.

There was no physical movement to indicate it, only a gasp, and he was dead. Precisely at that moment, Reet stooped in the doorway and looked inquiringly into the hut. His timely coming coincided with the climax of my joy, and I cried out, "Reet, Yuol has just died. He has just gone to God."

We left Yuol and closed the wooden door behind us. The old woman sat down outside. Other patients sitting by the huts stopped their talking as we walked by. They could tell Yuol had died, and they wanted to ignore it, turning their backs on death as one does when a gust of wind blows dust into the air.

It was the family's responsibility to bury their own dead, but since Yuol was far from his family, someone else would have to do it. Burial was not a simple matter. To the Nuer people, death is as contagious as smallpox. Consequently much precaution is taken when death comes. No one outside the family would volunteer to bury the dead without being covered by the payment of one cow from the deceased's family, as one is covered with a life insurance policy. Young men inside the family leave the burying to the older men and to the women if at all possible. They flee from it as one flees a poisonous snake or a rabid animal.

Kuac had been to see Yuol while he was sick but he was not there when he died. But after we had left the body, Reet went back to Kuac and with a third man, another believer, the three of them buried old Yuol. They were not afraid of death or of God. There was no payment to cover them.

They dug the grave across the river, under the bamboos where the earth was soft. Kuac, whose travels outside the tribe enabled him to see how other people did things, said that they would begin a new custom that day and dig a shelf at the bottom of the grave as the Shilluk do, under which they would place the head to protect it. It was April and hot, but the heat was of little concern to them; they were concerned that this grave be the finest they had ever made. For once, it seemed, something other than an earthly tradition or tribal custom united them. This unity seemed to include even me. I think the men recognized it, too, for when the grave was ready they said, "Go, bring him." I brought Yuol across the river, in the motor boat with Man Gaac and Reet's wife, and another man, a relative of Yuol's, who had been in the village. He was wrapped in the white cloth, lying on his sleeping skin, his body "emptied" of its bracelets, beads, and hair. We brought him up the riverbank to the grave where the women took off the cloth, folded his legs in the fetal position, and the men lowered him into the grave. "Give me the cloth," Kuac said, and he covered him with it as Yuol had asked.

Then we got down on our knees and pushed the dirt into the hole, tramping it solidly to secure it from hyenas, until the hole was full and the slight rise on the leaf-covered floor was all that marked the grave. In a year's time even that would be gone, for the river would rise and the water would overflow into the bamboo grove, leveling the grave with the land around.

We stood by the grave and sang, "Jehovah Jesus Is My Shepherd," after which Kuac took the Nuer translation of St. John's Gospel from the back pocket of his khaki shorts and read the first few verses of the fourteenth chapter:

"Don't let your heart worry, you believe God, so believe me also. The hut of my Father has many places, if this were not so I would have told you. I am going to make ready a place for you. When I get the place ready for you, I will come back. I will take you as my people, because the place where I live, you will live there too. The place where I go, you know the path to it."

Kuac asked Reet to pray, and when he finished we picked up the digging tools and slid back down the bank to the boat at the river's edge.

Death had come. Our hands had touched and handled it. We saw in it our own end and we were not afraid, for love had been there and in its presence were peace and hope.

17

AND YE SHALL BE AS GODS

Sunday after Sunday, Kuac stood before the people in his white robe, preaching the Word of God. The church was now his responsibility and was no longer under the mission's care. This was fine at first, until the momentum of school days wore away, and the glory dimmed, and there was instead the lonely plodding on an untested, unfamiliar road.

The biggest problem by far to emerge, swamping everything else into insignificance, was how he was going to live and support his family. For not only was he responsible for himself and his wife, but all of his relatives came to him for help because they knew he received a salary. He did not plant a field any more or go fishing because, for the last ten years, he had been clothed and fed and subsidized by the mission and government, so that slowly, almost imperceptibly, he had been eased into a new economy where the all-important need was money. Now he found himself with no steady income and no hope of any, dependent upon people whose money supply, he knew, was tied up in one corner of their cloth, or hidden somewhere in a little can. Each Sunday the offering was received, but the level of the coins kept dropping in the treasury, and Kuac's salary commitment was being only partially met.

Settled now in the role of pastor, he watched his contemporaries who, following their schooling, had found employment with the government, the main employer of the entire south Sudan. These men were on the government wage escalator and with each raise in pay they rose in prestige. Out of his conditioned sense of what was the honorable attitude for a Christian to take, Kuac vowed in the early days that money was of little consequence to him, that what he wanted was to preach the Gospel to his people; and unrealistically, we encouraged him in it. At the same time, his new sense of the rightness of things, which we also encouraged, led him to spend his money for clothes, shoes, eating bowls, blankets, soap, and the like for all of his family; and to satisfy his newly acquired tastes, introduced to him by his teachers upon whom was the burden to enlighten Africa's people, he spent more money on sugar, tea, cooking oil, onions, salt, and necessities such as charcoal for his iron, kerosene and spare parts for his lantern, besides giving money to his family to buy grain, milk, medicine, and to pay their taxes.

Then in the thatch-roofed church he asked the people to bring more money, or if not that, to bring eggs which the missionaries would buy. At best this would not be enough to meet the deficit, but the white men had directed him to do this, supporting themselves by the Scripture, and he made the effort to follow their suggestion. However, respect for his people gradually overpowered him and he said to me one day, "Nyarial, asking the people for money is not good. I cannot keep on doing it."

The realization that his own living, and that of his family, depended upon the handful of people in the church mounted in his mind. He knew there was no hope of sustained giving by them. He also knew the white man had no plan for him other than to insist that the people must learn to give, willy-nilly. It was another of those areas where the white man dictated what was to be done from behind the Bible without having to submit to the discipline involved himself. It was a kind of imprisonment where freedom could be had only by trusting God to create money where there was no money.

Ideally, Kuac was to find his joy and ambition for living as a pastor, but he was under pressure to become something he knew very little about. He was like an actor playing a part. To the white people he was "Pastor Moses." He was sent to official church meetings in distant towns and countries as a symbol of the new church in the south Sudan. Distances were far and travel costly, but Presbytery

paid the bill. At first this traveling was exciting to him, but in time
he had no desire to go. He would climb into the plane like a com-
muter on his way to work. He was like a grafted branch that did not
take. He was a cog in a machine which he did not understand. He
was supposed to be something which was out of his reach; he was
supposed to produce and he could not do it. He did not have the
will, because the vision was not his. However, he was not blind. He
did see. What he saw discouraged him.

He saw that the civilized world wanted nothing from him or
his people. He knew that his people had nothing to give that world.
He knew they were despised. To that world he bore their shame,
not pitifully, but resentfully. Why was their way of life not equally
justifiable as any other man's?

He referred to this on one occasion. It was on Christmas day.
The little group of Christians from around the mission were sitting
in Reet's barn, on the floor which had been swept clean and animal
skins laid upon it, ready to enjoy a feast of *kisera,* the unleavened
Arab bread and stew. While the women were preparing the food, the
men talked freely together, discussing the poles holding up the barn
roof—where they had come from, what kind of tree each one was,
how far it had been carried from the forest, how heavy it was, and
which ones had been used in former barns; all of that and the fate of
a certain village dog which had been downed by a spear, thrown by
one of Reet's neighbors, because it had been killing sheep in the area.

As soon as the women brought the food, we all sat together and
after Reet had prayed, thanking God that we could eat together like
this—men and women—and not be afraid, and thanking Him for
the food, and for Reet's little son whose birth we were celebrating
as well as Christmas, we began to eat.

It was after we had eaten—every bowl was empty and not a
drop remained; the women had brought soap and water for us to
wash our hands—and after refreshing glasses of hot, sugary tea,
that Kuac turned to me and said, "Nyarial, what would the men of
your country think if they could come now in an airplane and see

you here like this? Would they not think you were a fool being here with us simple people?"

His question was apropos of nothing and came with an abruptness which triggered in my mind the memory of riding on the postboat on the Nile as a young missionary with a white woman, an official's wife, who, upon hearing that I was expecting to spend my life in the Sudan, reacted violently. Looking down on the barge below us where the black travelers sat lazily in the sun, and with a great sweep of her white arm out over them, she said, "If I were you, I'd let them rot!"

I did not deny that Kuac was right. And I told him so. But the fact remained that in the heart of this African was a burden too heavy to bear. He was saying in effect, Why don't they accept us the way we are? We had gathered that day to commemorate the birth of Christ and God's love for us, and yet Kuac, the only educated one in the group, whose eyes had been opened, knew that between us—the white man and the Nuer—there was a strange gulf fixed. He was beginning to know the weight of the serpent's utterance, "And ye shall be as gods, knowing good and evil."

The next year Kuac and Nyatiac had their first child, a son. According to custom everything associated with a newborn child is the women's responsibility, including the giving of its name. The child was always near the women—its mother, its grandmother, its sister—who carried it, held it, nursed it, washed it, slept beside it. But little John, Kuac's son, belonged to his father from the start. Kuac named him John Ruac. John was for the disciple of Jesus and Ruac meant "talk," and referred in this case to the "talk of God," the Bible, many portions of which Kuac had translated. Kuac cared for the child more meticulously than a woman would have done. He carried the baby in his arms to the clinic for periodic checkups and prophylactic injections, with Nyatiac walking at his side. The older women laughed at him and called him *turuk*, which meant foreigner, because he would do this, refusing to follow the Nuer custom of the woman carrying the child in a basket on her head. But what people thought did not bother Kuac.

He told his wife that John was "his child," that is, his responsibility, explaining to her that she did not know how to care for him properly, that by observing Kuac she would learn, and the next child would be "hers." He made a bed with screening around the sides and put a muslin mosquito net on the top to keep away the flies. He bought boiled milk at the mission and cereal to supplement the baby's diet. He did not allow the women to take things into their own hands if the child showed any discomfort. They dare not take out the baby's teeth still hidden beneath the gums, for example. Instead, Kuac would take John to the doctor.

Kuac did allow the little boy to look like a Nuer. From the very beginning his head was shaved, except for the usual topknot on the crown, and he wore beads around his ankles. Soon he learned his name and, like his mother, would burst into smiles when someone called to him. Nyatiac pinched his cheeks, kissed his puckered mouth and sang lullabys to him, holding him on her lap, dancing him on her knee, saying, "John! John!" until his laughter began spilling all over. John grew and was loved and was strong.

At the same time, Kuac's personal problems intensified. His credit at the local merchants was no longer honored. He had borrowed all he could from the missionaries and because he wanted more, the relations between him and them were strained. He was worried and listless, and had lost heart in his preaching. The pressure upon him now was one of enforced sacrifice. The role created for him had raised him to an office of high standing above his fellows in the village, but of less standing than that of most of his contemporaries in the government's employ. He was very much aware of this and measured himself, his salary, and other benefits against theirs. He was not satisfied, but he held tenaciously to his place in society. A precedent was established when he was always taken by plane or car to the places Presbytery sent him. But the day came when a missionary of the Presbytery told him to walk, and when he got to the place, to sleep on the floor. In the missionary's mind any man of God should be willing to do this; he certainly would—and in doing so become a hero. But to Kuac it meant losing face, and he refused to go. This made the missionaries wrinkle their brows and wonder what had happened to Moses Kuac.

In time he was made moderator of the Presbytery. He came to my house one morning shortly before he was to go to the meeting in Malakal and said to me, "I do not want to go to the Presbytery meeting."

I looked at him across from me in the wicker chair where he always sat when we translated. His hair was cut and combed; his face smooth and sharply outlined by the bones of his cheeks and jaw. His short-sleeved blue shirt was tucked neatly into his belted khaki shorts and no ornaments adorned him—only the six telltale horizontal initiation scars across his forehead, and the empty holes in his ear lobes marked him as a Nuer tribesman. He had replaced the conventional Nuer costume with Western dress and done it well, with dignity and simplicity, without the usual gawdy, cheap trappings—the plastic comb, the wristwatch, the dark glasses, the fountain pen, the plastic wristband. Gone from him was the aura of romanticism and mystery still surrounding his brethren, which enchants the twentieth-century traveler seeing them from the river steamer on the Nile. He appeared to be something else now, something more to the civilized man's liking and understanding.

"But aren't you the moderator?" I said, aware of his feelings.

"*Uh.*"

"Well, then, why don't you want to go? I think you should go. It is not good if you don't, Kuac. The men will not agree to it."

He did not answer. His jaw was set. His lips were tight. His face was troubled, as it had been off and on for months.

"It is a thing of uselessness," he said. "The government peeks around us to see what the white men are doing."

"But you are the head of the Presbytery. Why does the government look at the white men?"

"Does the government accept us? They do not accept the black men. We are nothing to them. What is the moderator? The white men tell us what to do." Kuac did not use the term "black men" derogatorily. The Nuer called themselves very proudly, "we, the black people," and told us white people how bad it was that we had not been born with black skin.

It was true. When the white men said, Don't you think you should have a Bible conference? the black men thought so. And when they said, There are many southerners in the north Sudan, don't you think you should send a pastor up there to teach them? they thought so. And when the white men said a letter had come from New York, from the people of the church there, saying an All-African Conference was to be held in Nigeria, and did the black men not wish to send a delegate? they thought they should.

Then when the white men asked the black men what they thought about how to get the money to do these things, the black men said they had no money, they thought it should come from Presbytery. And the white men said they must remember that the church had its obligation and must learn to meet it, else it could not be strong; but they were all brothers and they would supplement what the black men had because of the love between them which came from God.

So arrangements were made, money was provided, the plane was sent, and the black men were moved across the Sudan like checkers on a board.

Who was to deny that the white men told the black men what to do? And yet who was to tell Kuac that if the white men did not do this the Presbytery would not function as it was supposed to?

"I do not know, Nyarial," he continued, "I am tired of it."

"What are you tired of?"

"I want a holiday. My body is tired. I have never had a holiday. I have been a pastor for two years with no holiday. Is this good?"

It was March. Fire, the Nuer called it. The hottest, driest, deadest month in the year. Outside the screen window a black-and-white crow made its rachet-sounding noise high in the smooth-limbed acacia tree. It was an irritating sound from a loathsome bird whose kind came in droves in the dry season, and sat in the treetops like aerial bishops, bickering and scrapping with each other over bits of fish and garbage scavenged from the ground.

I looked out at the yard, now a slab of baked earth, void of life and bleached by the white, white light of the sun. I looked through the naked hedge and across the river to the huts shimmering along the river bank, and across the plain to the horizon. I could see the cattle grazing under the sun and I could hear a man singing far away. And I thought, That man has his troubles, but I haven't caused them, nor does he need me to solve them. He does not read or write, he does not wear clothes, but he has something to sing about. I looked back at Kuac and said, "There is nothing which I know about your holiday. Do you get a holiday?"

Does not Mr. ——— have a holiday? Is he not a pastor?"

"Yes."

I knew he was thinking of how the white man took his family on holiday to Egypt or Kenya or Ethiopia.

"And my bicycle, why can I not have a new bicycle? I am going to see Mr. ——— and tell him everything that is wrong with it."

"Was not your bicycle his gift to you?" I said.

"*Uh*, three years ago while I was still in divinity school. And now the tires are smooth, the spoke is broken and it stops poorly. The seat is old, and the wheels, they do not run well. Many parts are bad on it."

It was not like Kuac to complain, but lately nothing satisfied him. He had wanted electricity in his house. Did not the servants on another mission station have electricity, he had asked. "But your house is not wired," I had reminded him. "It costs money to wire a house and put up the poles."

"Do you not have the money?" he had asked.

"No, not for this."

"How can this be?"

"You will have to believe me."

And if you did have electricity, I thought to myself, could you pay for it every month? No. But I cannot say this to you. It frustrates and cheapens you. It is part of the reason why you said to me once, "Pray for me that I do not commit suicide."

"Do you have money for the lorry ride to Malakal?" I said.

"No, I have no money. You will give it to me and you will get it back from Presbytery."

"Okay."

I took out a one-pound note and wrote it down in my book.

"I will bring the money back with me, my sister," he said as he went out. "Remain in peace."

"Go in peace, Kuac," I said.

It was not so hot inside under the thatch, but the typewriter, the metal table, the pencils, the ink bottle, the chair were all warm to the touch, and my arm, where it rested on the table, peeled from the table's surface like the paper on a decal. I sat looking at the account book. Money. A blessing and a curse, and in this country; at this time, mostly a curse. It is possible to live without money, I thought, but you have to be content with far less. Still, to be content is to be content, and there is no argument, the Nuer people have been as content as any people. It is not they who have agitated for a change.

I sat up in my chair and leaned my elbow on the table, propping my head in the palm of my hand, and began to doodle with a pencil. Is it not immoral, I thought, to overpower people against their will, without their invitation or consent, thrusting oneself upon them in the guise of goodness?

We were missionaries. We had meant only to bring people the Gospel: salvation, and the benefits of the Gospel: love, peace, joy, and freedom from the fear of death. But our possessions came with us, our trucks, our motor boats, our electricity. These were the things we were using to evangelize. At least it was in this term that we justified their existence. We did not foresee that our things would become more important to the people than our Gospel, that they would want *them.* No one was to be blamed for this, but as it was turning out, were we not becoming more of a stumbling block than a help to the people?

I cupped my chin in the palm of my hand and looked out the window. A man with a big black catfish on his head with its tail reaching halfway down the man's back was walking by on the path. Has there ever been an example in history, I thought, where a nation set out to make leaders in another nation to ensure the second nation's development? I did not know, but the idea seemed strange and unworkable to me. Still, as a mission, this was our formula: to train men to be Christian leaders and work ourselves out of a job. Don't leaders come from within the group, the result of a common unrest and desire to move forward in a single direction? Have we not taken too much for granted in presuming that the people want to be led, and that we know the way they should go? Are we willing to assume the responsibility for the lives of these people?

An old man went by on the path. He was bent and walked with a staff. His head was covered with a scrap of cloth, protecting him from the sun. His feet were bare. He walked slowly, feeling his way. I knew him and had always pitied him. He could scarcely see. He had no nose. It had been eaten away by yaws. The cloth on his head was one of mine; he came to me periodically for a new one when what he had was of no more use. His speech was impaired, but this did not prevent him from talking. He laughed when he talked and rubbed his bony hand across his shiny balding head. He lived by himself and kept his field, and in the fall he would come with a gift of corn with the husks pulled back and tied together. Then he would ask for a razor blade and go away, saying, "It is good, my daughter." Perhaps he was not to be pitied after all.

But these who were being weaned from the earth to a money economy in a land where the employer is the government, where jobs are far away and scarce, where the people themselves have no vision, no capital to create their own jobs—it is these who are to be pitied.

A little boy with very long thin legs appeared outside the window and pressed his nose against the screen.

"Nyarial," he said in a tiny voice, "this paper." Lifting his hand he showed me a split straw he was holding with a piece of paper tucked into it.

I said to him, "Go to the door," and he ducked away to the front screen door where I met him and took the paper and read it.

"Nyarial," it said, "I want fifty piasters for food for my wife while I am gone. Give them to Luk. I will go at two o'clock. It is I, Kuac."

I hesitated, as though Kuac were standing there, then went and got the money and took it to Luk.

"Hold them well in your hand, my child," I said, clenching my fist together as a demonstration to him. "Don't let them be lost."

He looked up at me solemnly and answered softly, *"Uh."* Then he turned and half ran, half walked down the path and out the gate.

I went back to my table and wrote in the book "fifty piasters" under the sums already accumulated there. It was a snowball which was soon to fall apart.

18

A LEOPARD TAMED

The men of Presbytery became concerned about Kuac. They made a visit to Nasir to encourage him. Two decisions were made: that he should cease from the work of translating (for which he received a separate salary from the mission) because it was impinging on his pastoral duties; and that a study should be built for him near the church. His house, which had been the combined effort of mission and church people, had become a rendezvous for relatives and villagers, so a large thatch hut was built by Presbytery with screened windows and a proper door, and Kuac moved in with his books, a table, and two chairs, and the stipulation that no one was allowed to sleep there.

But this did not answer his problem. The debts he owed overburdened him and broke his spirit. The knowledge he had of a hostile world threatened him. He was finding how impregnable was the wall between him and his people; that preaching the Gospel was not a guarantee that men would be won to Christ. He was also bucking the questions his own culture asked God, for which he had no answers—that is, he could offer his people Jesus Christ, but he could not promise them children or food. He was seeing that even in the Sudan, in spite of the white man's insistence that all Christians were one in Christ, the Evangelical Church in the north did not welcome the southern tribesmen. This was a shock to him. This "Christian" world that he had been invited into and given a place in was now becoming a disillusionment to him. The people he knew best, his own age group, who were educated and baptized and held positions in the church organization, disappointed him. In their rush to become civilized they were eager for power. Away from their villages at government posts where mission stations were often located, working as Christian medical dressers, teachers, clerks, these men were a marked minority and treated with special favor by the missionaries, who gave them positions in the local church and listened to them on church matters. As time went on it was with these educated men that the church organization was constructed. But there was often a dichotomy in their lives, where in the vital affairs of life and death concerning themselves and their families, the gods of their fathers still claimed their first allegiance. A letter came to my hands one time which was written by one of these educated churchmen. He was a government medical dresser writing to the head chief at Nasir. It was a typewritten letter dated, "Governor's Office, Malakal."

Dear Chief Puur Deet Buop,

Is it good peace, chief? We are all at peace here, we who live in Malakal.

Chief, I have something I say to you. I have heard that Pal Thoaan took a calf after I left, the calf was the one we had anointed with ashes for God, we the family of Thoaan. I have heard that the calf was later given as payment of a fine by order of the chief, and now it is said that the mother-of-Cuol is sick, Child-of-Buop [this is another way to address the chief]. Now I ask you, how can this be good?

Chief, if you must fine Pal—the boy who has a god—that calf which you took, let it be returned to the ashes because that is the reason why mother-of-Cuol is now sick.

If it was the other chief, Bol Kuany, who gave it, ask him to let it be returned to the ashes, and if it was one of the lesser chiefs tell them to let it be returned now.

I am very sad that mother-of-Cuol should die because of Pal. I did not know we had fallen out, I and Pal, that he would allow a cow of God to be used for a fine payment behind my back. What I really feel is if Pal wants the cattle, I will come and we will discuss what we will do. To me, he is my child and he cannot bring death to my hearth.

If the marriage cattle for Nyapar have not yet been given, if he wants to keep the cattle, he cannot do it. Even you yourself, Puur, you were not the person who finalized the marriage of Nyapar. That the cattle have not been given you know very well.

If you, Chief Puur Deet, see that the body of mother-of-Cuol is ill, put her and my wife on the boat and send them to me and I will inject them. Then they will return. But if it is a sickness of God because that calf was taken, let it be set apart with ashes again for Him. Let the returning of the calf be that which turns God's heart back again [that is, causes God to repent of what He has done in afflicting the old woman].

One more thing, I have bought you a brown-and-black-colored walking stick. I put an ivory ring on its top and one on its bottom. I gave it to Ruac Kong, the wife of Kuek, to give to you. I bought it for you.

Sleep well. I am, Cuol Thoaan.

To Kuac, who was the sole pastor in his tribe, the pioneer upon whom the future of the church rested, this dichotomy in the men representing the church presented an indefinable situation. He was not upheld by the warm spirit of a group committed to the evangelization of the tribe. There was no strength from within to encourage him and goad him on. He became increasingly discouraged and showed less and less interest in pastoral duties, which prompted another visit from Presbytery.

The missionary who came brought with him a little notebook, and together he and Kuac sat along the riverbank one afternoon, discussing the use of the book. It was lined and had various headings on each page where Kuac was to indicate each day whether he had had morning devotions, Bible study, done visitation, sermon preparations, and the like. Following their time together, I asked the missionary if he had been able to help Kuac.

"I never got through to him," he replied.

What was to be the last Presbytery-sponsored trip Kuac made while I was still in Africa was to Nigeria, as one of the three delegates from the two presbyteries in the Sudan, to the All-African Christian Conference there. He was waiting in my house until the plane came so that I could take him to the airstrip. He was wearing his gray striped trousers and white nylon shirt a missionary had given him and that he had had for years. At the early hum of the plane's coming he stood up, impeccably neat and clean in his old clothes, picked up his small brown suitcase, which was empty except for some papers and books, and said, "Nyarial, take care of John and Nyatiac while I am gone. Maybe you can go and see how they are getting along sometimes."

I said I would.

In the notebook in the glove compartment of the Jeep I wrote the date, the mileage, and the nature of the trip I was about to make: Kuac—airstrip—Nigeria meeting, and put my initials. The use of the Jeep would be paid for by Presbytery.

On the way to the airstrip, which was one mile from the mission station, I asked Kuac about his clothes, if what he was wearing was all he had for the journey. Yes, he said, it was, but he understood they were to buy clothes for him when he got to Khartoum.

At the strip he got in the plane and strapped himself in. I told him to be sure to see the ocean. Then he was gone.

When he came back he had seen the ocean and was thrilled. He had also ridden in an elevator and his stomach had done strange things. The people of Ibadan and Lagos amazed and startled him; he was discouraged by their progress.

The conference, he said, was all right, but the Presbytery had not given the three delegates enough spending money. They all agreed on that.

I asked him if he had discussed polygamy with any of the other pastors. No, he said, he hadn't. He had not talked with anyone except a white man from New York who naively promised him schooling in America if Kuac would write to him later about it. That was the most important aspect of the entire trip. Kuac wrote that letter immediately, full of hope. He asked me to correct his writing. But the answer, of course, came back that unfortunately it was not possible for Kuac to come at this time. This made no sense whatsoever to Kuac except to underline what he had suspected for a long time, that the white man did not keep his word.

I did not know the pain of his dilemma until one morning, after the Nigerian trip, he met me in the garden. Standing as always head up, chest thrust forward and hands at his sides, he spoke my name once and then again, as in a question, signifying that he had something on his mind of more than ordinary weight. This and the fact that it was so early in the morning and not his usual time of coming, was enough to cause me to turn my complete attention to him as one does when anticipating the unburdening of a friend.

He looked down at his clothes, the khaki shorts and white nylon shirt that he was wearing, and said something like this:

"Nyarial, I am a poor man. There was not enough money to pay me this month, and there was not enough last month, either. Look at my clothes. They are old. When I go away, like to Nigeria, I am given new clothes. This is good. But is this the way I am to find my clothes? What about my family? Can I get a job? No. I cannot work for the government and be a pastor. The government would not agree. The Presbytery would not agree. My head is mixed up, Nyarial. I cannot find what I should do."

I looked at him, the moderator of the Presbytery, the symbol of the church in the south Sudan, and saw him there—a broken man. Lured across the cultural boundary of his society where he was superior to me, into my society he had lost his identity and become a pauper and a foreigner. What was now essential to him, he could not provide. He was, instead, dependent upon the white man, and his know-how, and his things. Those six thready scars across his forehead meant very little to him now. He had nothing to take their place.

I fumbled for words to say. We had been over some rough places recently as Kuac had battled to maintain his dignity, but now he had laid it aside and was coming for help as he used to come when life was full of happy surprises. But how could I help him? I was part of his problem, because I was partner to his "progress." I represented everything he wanted but could not have. So once again I found myself unable to help, and in my helplessness turned to God.

"Kuac," I said finally, "I know your trouble is big. It is not your trouble alone, but belongs to all the young men of your generation in this country who have left the way of the people. They have left one way, but there is no other way for them to go; no way that they know. I don't see the way to go, either, especially not here in the Sudan where you are so isolated and alone. But there is one thing I know. It is that you were born a Nuer man and this you must not despise. It is on your head to believe that this is what God wants you to be. This does not require clothes. If you live with clothes, that is good. If you live without clothes, that is good also. Both are the same. There is something more important than this. You know what it is. It is to live your life with all your heart for God. Like Jesus did. Only God can show you what that means. Then, one day, God Himself will show you a greater meaning of it all. That meaning is hidden now, the Bible says. If the wearing of clothes were important for this, God would give you clothes to wear. This is what I believe."

Then came the bitterest blow of all. Kuac had prayed and believed to see the blessing of God on his family. If God had been waiting for the past centuries for a man to arise among the Nuer people whose heart would be faithful toward Him, surely He recognized Kuac in this and would bless him. But when John was two years old he became sick with a mild case of measles which later developed into a croupy cough. For weeks he was never without medical care from both the doctor and the nurse at the mission clinic. But one afternoon, as he lay on his father's low wooden bed, his breathing weakened, and his mother who heard it, said with alarm, "What is it?"

His father, who sat beside him said, "He is dead."

Nyatiac wept.

Kuac stood beside the bed and looked down at the child. He stood for a long time before he pulled the cloth over him and went out. It did not make sense. Soap, injections, God—he had trusted them all.

The tools for digging the grave were in the mission storehouse. Kuac went out of the yard where a cluster of quiet women sat, and walked along the river path. It was midday. He walked quickly with his head down, passing others by. He stepped off the brick path and went along the side of it where the earth was smooth and cool under the trees. At the school playfield he left the path and walked back to the storehouse. The workman in charge looked up.

"It is you, Kuac?" he said.

"*Uh,* it is I. Give me the pick for digging."

The workman's eyes blinked. "What is it?" he said.

"The child is dead."

"*Ae,* thorry," the man said, using the Nuer version of the English word *sorry,* and lowered his eyes.

They began to dig beside the house, Kuac with the people helping him. It was March and the earth was like a rock. The women carried water on their heads from the river and poured it onto the ground to soften it. Kuac dug slowly, scooping out the earth with his hands. As the hole went deeper others helped him, on their knees, scooping out the earth, piling it along the sides, reaching down again with their arms, soiling their hands, muddying their bracelets, sweating fiercely in the sun. Down so far they did not need water any more, the earth was moist there and the hoe cut into it more easily.

Inside the house the women prepared the body, taking off the ankle bracelets, the string of tiny waist beads, and shaving away the black cap of hair on the child's head.

When the grave was ready Kuac said, "Go, bring the child."

They brought him on a sleeping skin and Kuac lowered him into the grave and tucked a small, white cloth around him. "Is that good?" he said.

"*Uh,*" it is good a woman said.

Some of the relatives began throwing in lumps of black clay.

"Where is Nyatiac?" someone asked.

"She is not coming."

"But how can she get pregnant again?" a woman said, for Nuer belief held that the dead child's mother must participate in the burial if she is ever to have another child.

No one answered.

The men continued to wad the moist clay and throw it heavily into the hole, and to tramp it down solidly with their bare heels.

"Is it not good?" a man said as he traced the outline of the grave with his feet, stomping it down as he went.

"*Uh*, it is good," someone answered.

When all of the dirt was back in the hole, and a small mound marked the grave, Kuac dusted off his hands and went into the house and came back with his Bible. The sun was red in the west. The air was hot and still. Crows cawed pitilessly in the bare branches of the trees. People, chattering back and forth, walked along the path. Someone called across the river for a canoe.

Nyatiac sat with the women next to the table, piled with enamel bowls. Her cheeks were smeared with tears, her breast heaved with stifled sobs. Kuac opened his Bible to the Old Testament, and began translating from it the words of King David's lament for his son: "O my son, Absalom, my son. My son, Absalom! Would God I had died for thee, O Absalom, my son, my son!"

Then he closed the book and explained how he had loved John, but that God took him. But, he said, he was not afraid. He believed he would see John one day, when everyone rose up out of death, as the Word of God said would happen. Then he prayed, and when he finished he said, "This is the end," and the handful of people got up and began walking quietly away. A man said, "I go to bathe." A woman began to stir up the fire. Nyatiac stayed sitting and Kuac went into the house.

I was not there when this happened. I pictured it from the letter Kuac sent me. He wrote, "The hearts of Nyatiac and me were very, very sad. We loved John so much that, at the time, we thought it would not matter if God never gave us another child. We thought that John can never be replaced." A Nuer child when it dies is forgotten. Another child, if born, takes it place. Often this child is named Cuol, which means the one who has replaced the dead child. Kuac was not prepared to forget John. He wanted to remember him. Neither was he afraid of the death which John brought into the family, which the birth of another child would remove. Although he could not understand why God had taken his child, he had not been left desolate. He was free from the bondage of the fear of death, free to remember, and free to believe.

19

WHO HATH BELIEVED OUR REPORT?

The Arab military government, which took control of the civilian government in 1958, reserved its own kind of pressure for men like Kuac. Shortly after John died, Kuac was put in prison. This and the first imprisonment (which had taken place some months before) were surrounded with mystery, and were of short duration. If for no other purpose they were meant to engender fear in Kuac, in the Christians, and in the villagers of the area. Utterly confident of their popularity among the southerners at the time of independence, the northern Arabs came to know within a few short years that they were badly mistaken. The southerners distrusted them. They remembered the slave trade and the ivory bracelets taken from the severed arms of their forefathers.

The Arabs, overanxious to turn the Sudan into a Muslim state, declared Friday, the Muslim holy day, to take the place of the Christian Sunday, and in the southern elementary schools took the vernacular languages out of the curriculum and substituted Arabic. The southerners bitterly resented this. In the local courts chiefs were pressured into becoming Muslim, and they, in turn, favored those villagers who spoke patronizingly of the government. Muslim holy men, like missionaries, were brought into the south to teach the Quran in the public schools, and to start Quranic schools for boys. Gradually restrictions were placed upon Christian mission activity, and secret police, themselves naive southerners looking for money, were employed to spy on any and all foreigners and citizens who might be insidiously at work, plotting against the government. In spite of the secret nature of the job, these men were publicly known, and one missionary introduced an African to a visitor from

America by saying, "This is so-and-so, he is the CID [secret police-men] here in Malakal." Many of them did not realize to what extent they would become traitors to their own people.

The deterioration in relationships between the north and the south reached its climax when southerners fled into other coun-tries to organize and arm themselves against the Arab army. They began a terrorizing, sniping warfare against the northern soldiers and government servants, teachers, and merchants living in the south. When this happened the government then began evicting the missionaries, blaming them for the southern revolt. The per-sonnel of the Sudan United Mission located on the west bank of the Nile south of Khartoum in the Nuba Mountains had almost been depleted when the first missionaries of the American Mis-sion were evicted in 1958. Then in December 1962, I was included in a group of eleven missionaries who were given their notices to be out of the country in six weeks' time. The notices had been mimeographed on legal size pieces of paper and were delivered to the mission headquarters in Malakal, where I happened to be on that Saturday afternoon, by a policeman who drove up in a government lorry at two o'clock just when all the government offices close.

The notice was from the Police Headquarters, Malakal, Upper Nile Province, and was dated Saturday, 8 December 1962. It said:

Dear Madam:

    I have been directed by the Director, Passports, Immigration and Na-tionality to inform you that you should leave the Sudan within six weeks from today, i.e. on or before Saturday 19th January 1963 for the fulfillment of the object for which you have been allowed to enter the Sudan.

    Please acknowledge receipt of this letter.

Yours faithfully,
COMMANDANT OF POLICE

I went back to Nasir on Monday and prepared to sell my things. The preparation for the sale and the sale itself proved to the people that I was indeed leaving. The sale was on Wednesday; I planned to leave Nasir on the following Friday. During that week I had visitors every day who came to sit, to talk, and to pray. It was like attending one's own wake. The same people came and went and came again. It was not a large group of people, but the few who came, came to be with me. Even as no man of them lives alone, so they never allow anyone to die alone. And they were treating me in the same way. I had not felt such warmth and kindness before as came from their simplicity and faithfulness. One old man I scarcely knew took the broom from my hand and swept the floor of my house. That was a woman's job, but he did it for me.

An old woman who saw a much-coveted oil can in the corner showed unusual restraint by saying, "Nyarial, I would never ask you for that can, but I just wondered what you were going to do with it?"

"It has no owner now," I said, "maybe you will agree to be its owner?"

"*Uh,*" she said quickly, "I will agree."

Man Nyagon, who was the neatest housekeeper in the world and could mud plaster a hut floor to resemble the smoothest cement, and who was also a friend of Man Gaac's (it was because of Man Gaac that Man Nyagon had become a believer), came the oftenest and stayed the longest. She was six feet tall and thin, and had a thin matting of hair all over her head which she would shave off as soon as it got too long, and a purple-dyed cloth which she wore like a toga over her tight, smooth, short skirt.

She and I had visited many times together in the brief time that I had known her and had talked about God, and her old husband and the problems he made for Man Nyagon and his younger wife—things which worried her. She liked to laugh and did so at herself and at her troubles with her husband; and she liked to sing, which is what she did to ward off the fear that came over her the day she decided to pull up the shrine she had made in her hut. She composed songs, too, and we sang them in the Bible class.

The day before I left Nasir, she came to my house in the morning, brought her empty water pot, and stayed all day. In the afternoon as the sun was dropping in the west she said, "The world has become night; I must go to the village."

There was little to be said by that time. We had prayed quite a few times already that day, as people had come and gone. To God they had said, "God, old Father, Nyarial is going away and we will stay. We will not meet again here on this earth. You will lead us and we will come together one day in the sky."

And to me they had said, "It is not good, Nyarial, that you are going away. We will not see your eyes again." Now as she left she shook my hand and said, "Remain in peace."

I stood on the veranda and watched her go to the river, with her water pot. There was a bare hedge between us and I did not intend her to see me standing there; but when she turned away from the river, which was now level with the bank, her water pot shining in the sun as she steadied it on top of her head, and started toward the village, she stopped, turned again in my direction, and said from across the hedge, "Nyarial, why do you watch me?"

"It is for no reason, old mother," I said, and went into the house. This kind of sentiment was foreign to her. It was ominous and mysterious.

She had another way of showing her feelings, a more practical, less emotional and more meaningful way. She came again early the next morning, at the cooing of the doves. I had been lying in bed, listening to the soft, liquid music from their pinkish-gray throats, trying to push away the thoughts of departure, when she clapped at my door. This time she would not come in. She was like a messenger on the move.

"Nyarial, my daughter," she said. "I have come. Last night in the middle of the night, I remembered something my head had forgotten before. Congo is going to marry. That explains my coming. I thought it is not good that Nyarial goes without knowing this. That is the end of my talk. Now I go."

I watched her go down the path and out the gate. Congo was her only son. He had never been too well. That he was marrying was the biggest thing which would ever happen in her life. This was family news. She was including me in the family. If she had forgotten to tell me I would never have been able to know it, and she would have blamed herself, saying, "I did her wrong." But as it was she had told me all. Now I could go and when she thought of Congo and of me her mind would be at rest.

The morning was going quickly. After breakfast Kuac came and we read the Bible together and prayed.

"Nyarial," he said, "it isn't the things we have done together that I will miss, but our talks together—I will miss that most. You must write to me. I need to learn many more things."

He could not know what a friend he had been to me. I trusted him completely in what he did and what he said. I thought of him as a man who loved Jesus Christ. He had been shaken and was yet to be shaken, perhaps more than his white teachers had ever contemplated or experienced themselves.

After he had gone, my thoughts of the early morning came back to me. For the educated African perhaps it was best that we go. Our presence frustrated them. Our possessions made them jealous and outshone the Gospel. It was not a matter of hiding our possessions, or living without them; everyone knew what we had, what our country had, whether they saw them or not. The radio told them, the press told them, the tourists told them. And more and more they resented us and wondered why we had kept them from having what we had.

For the village people, however, who were not trying to be like us, who were still content in being *nath*—the people, proud of their cattle and of themselves—perhaps we still had a useful function. But only God could be sure; only He knew what He meant when He said, "Go . . . and make disciples."

At eleven o'clock the plane was at the strip and I got in. Kuac and a few others were there. We sang, "Jehovah Jesus Is My Shepherd." He had proved this unmistakably to me.

The pilot got the all-clear sign for take-off and we taxied to the end of the strip. Then, given its freedom, the small plane raced down the dirt strip, billowing dust in its wake, and lifted into the sky. The hands of my friends waved goodbye, and their faces looked up at me as we roared past and left them standing there.

I looked down at the huts and barns dotting the plain. Not much had changed over the thirteen years since I had first come up the river, believing to see God work; nor over the sixty years since the first missionaries had come. A blanket of servile fear lay over the tribe. Light had not broken through the darkness. There were the paths criss-crossing the land. Over them the messages of good and evil still went. But not the Gospel. Generations had come and gone without hearing the Gospel, and without realizing that it was the Gospel: a message of Good News from God for them. The few who had heard of it had not all accepted it, but neither had they rejected it; it had never concerned them, even as I had never accepted or rejected heathenism.

Were the fields already white for harvest, and had we, or I, somehow failed?

I had buoyed my sinking spirits many times with the assurance that in spite of everything else God would certainly bless the translation work. This was *His* Word. He would see to its successful conclusion for His own sake and for the sake of the Nuer people. To not believe this was sin, I thought, because I was positive the translation work was synonymous with the will of God for me.

But I left knowing that in all probability the translation Kuac and I had done would be very short-lived. All of our work had been printed in the Roman script, but the Roman script was no longer being taught in the schools. Furthermore, the government had banned the vernacular languages as well, insisting that in order to unify the country everyone must speak only Arabic. The mission had submitted to the government an amplified and modified Arabicized alphabet for the vernaculars, but it was refused.

Would the Lord spurn forever and never again be favorable?

Had His steadfast love forever ceased? Were His promises at an end for all time?

Had the Lord forgotten to be gracious?

I was glad the psalmist could ask God those questions, because I was asking them too. They came because I had believed God to do something and He had not done it. I did not know why. I only knew one thing: that my feet were on a Rock, and the Rock never moved.

Why was this?

I could retrace the steps in my thinking to two times in my life when from the Word of God shafts of light were beamed directly at me. The first time was in my second term, when I was teaching the Gospel of John in a Bible class that met early in the morning, and we came to the place where the people said to Jesus, "And what must we do that we might work the works of God?"

And Jesus said, "This is the work of God, that ye believe in Him whom He hath sent."

I recognized the economy of what Jesus said, that He summed everything up in Himself, but I was sure, nevertheless, that I was to believe Him to *act* when it came to prospering the translation work and the efforts of evangelism.

But many years later, in view of the fact that my work apparently was not prospering, as I pursued the question of what exactly God did want of me, I found in Isaiah God's own words.

"Ye are my witnesses, saith the Lord, and my servant whom I have chosen that ye may know, and believe me, and understand that I am he." This is what He wanted of me. This is what was needful. Not the salvation of the Nuer people. Not the translation. No, it was something even greater than these. It was the severest test of faith I knew: to believe Him, not for what He would do, for that is only one infinitesimal aspect of God, but for who He is. It bespeaks the kind of faith that walks on water where there is no path—not only no direction, but no sense of gain, simply a measurement of the adequacy of my own knowledge of Him. The kind of knowledge which says:

Though the fig tree do not blossom,
 nor fruit be on the vines,
the produce of the olive fail
 and the fields yield no food,
the flock be cut off from the fold
 and there be no herd in the stalls,
yet I will rejoice in the Lord,
 I will joy in the God of my salvation.

Now as I left, I knew for myself, at least, that God meant what He had said: that I was to know, to believe, to understand that God is God, and leave His defense up to Him.

In February 1964, when the Sudan government ordered all remaining missionaries out of the south Sudan, Kuac was in prison again. As the mission Jeep with the soldier guards on it drove past the prison, taking the missionaries on their final journey to Malakal, Kuac stood in the yard looking out through the wire fence, waving goodbye. During that year, Kuac was beaten, put in chains, and solitary confinement. Of the situation at Nasir at the time of his arrest, and of his time in prison, he wrote:

When the young men fled [he refers to the young men of the tribe] because they refused the talk of the government, hunger became very strong with them, and they had no guns to fight the army with. So when they became so hungry they came back into the villages with their spears and took the guns away from the government policemen, and took away the grain and cloth from the merchants' shops, and they also killed some of the people.

When the government officials heard of this they became very frightened, and they came and put me back in prison. It was the worst imprisonment I had, and the longest, and the people thought I would be killed after the missionaries had gone. It is true many Christians in the prison were killed, some of whom even I saw die. Nyatiac, when she brought me food to the prison, was often slapped by the guards and cursed. She was very sad and discouraged, and very, very afraid. She suffered more than I did.

My suffering in the cell for twelve months taught me many important lessons concerning my Christian life. I suffered severely from mosquitoes, bed bugs, scorpions from the roof, snakes by night, rain and wind, cold and heat, threatening and abusing, torturing and killings and even the worst cell in which I had been for the five month period from June to November, the month I left the prison. Yet in spite of all this, God had not failed me. This is my voice of need every day while in the prison cell: Lord, keep me faithful and make me all that I can be in Jesus, and when I die, I shall meet you in Jesus, holding Him in my hand like a ticket for going into your presence.

Kuac was released in November 1964, and returned from the prison in Malakal to his home at Nasir for the next few months until his life became in danger again. In desperation because they could not bring order out of the chaos in the south Sudan, the military government decided to purge the land of educated southerners in order to regain control of the country. Teachers, medical dressers, pastors, clerks—any and all influential southerners were in danger of their lives. Hundreds and hundreds were killed and their bodies thrown into the Sobat and the Nile. Villages were attacked by armed soldiers, innocent people were slaughtered, and a general exodus of frightened, bewildered people ensued.

Kuac wrote of this purge:

"Murdering began in Nasir in June 1965 and until now [January 1966]. There is much murdering and killing. You remember that the little chapel at Nasir is near the army camp [the army had appropriated some of the school buildings to house their men at the mission], so this is where they capture most of the people. We pray and ask God to help us, but there is no answer. Yet we will continue in making much prayer to the Lord."

There was no choice but that he flee the country with his family, which now included his wife and a new baby, whom Kuac named James but the people called Cuol. They crossed the border on foot into neighboring Ethiopia where thousands of refugees had already gone, and are now living on a mission station in Nuer territory. From there he wrote me this letter in August 1966:

Is it peace, my sister, Nyarial?

We are at peace, all of us here.

You and I have delayed. We have not written to each other. It has been something like five months with no letters between us. I wrote the last letter, but you have not answered it. I do not know what has happened to you, but I believe you have not found anything bad during those months.

We met, I and your brother, at Dembi Dolo, the place of the church meeting in April. My heart was torn by its love; it was as though I had seen you. You look alike, you and your brother.

Tell my greetings to your family. Tell them, "I remember and think of you even as I remember and think of Nyarial, your daughter."

We have a small school here where the children are taught the language of the Ethiopians. I translate what the teacher says to the boys, and I teach myself together with the boys. I read a book in the language now. We had this teacher for two months only, then this Ethiopian boy, who was the teacher, was replaced by another Ethiopian who came here today to our village. These Ethiopians are nice people, not like the people of the Sudan.

We have heard that ———— stands before the people of God now at Nasir, and that many people go to the house of God. And we also heard that he treats his wife badly. He wants to divorce her. He himself has made two girls pregnant. He wants to take back the cattle from his wife's family so that he can marry one of the pregnant girls with them. We must beseech God very much for her because her heart is sad for having no child, and for this which wants that she leave the home of her husband.

Man Lul and Man Gaac are all in the Sudan.

Reet and his family are at this place. They are at peace. But Reet's cattle have not yet been released by the Gaaguang Nuer. Those cattle of Reet's were commandeered last year by those people called Gaaguang.

My wife, Nyatiac, gave birth to a boy-child on April 27, 1966 and we called his name Bi Kaan ["you will be rescued"], because Jesus rescued us out of many troubles, and we believe he will protect us from other troubles like these which are still ahead.

Nyatiac says, "Are you at peace, my sister? I have given birth again to a boy-child. I love you, Nyarial."

The wife of Duer says, "Are you at peace? Our brother Duer [her husband] has died."

. . . I went to Pi Lual, a place for refugees. I washed [baptized] one hundred and sixty heads on two days of God. These are people with not too strong a faith because they have troubles all of the time. The people of Pi Lual are many, reaching to 5000. . . . Many of the Nuer people in this country have hard hearts; they refuse to believe in Jesus. But God is stronger. He will call them on the day he says.

This time is a bad time for all the children. Most of them are caught by whooping cough. Our two children have the cough. There is no medicine for them now. . . .

Our country is full of rumors and troubles. Plead with God for us as you did when you lived here, my sister.

Sleep well, Nyarial, my sister. I am your brother, Kuac Nyoat.

EPILOGUE

Ten years have passed since all missionaries were finally evicted in 1964 from the southern Sudan. In the interim a guerrilla-type war was waged throughout the southern provinces. Thousands of refugees fled to Uganda, Ethiopia, and Zaire while school buildings, mission hospitals, clinics, churches, and other buildings were burned out or razed to the ground. Roads deteriorated from lack of use and care; airfields, once a source of pride throughout the south, became overgrown and disappeared. The southern provinces were shoved back into the stone age again.

No one will ever know how many southerners died. But during this war, which raged simultaneously with the war in Viet Nam, it is estimated that somewhere between three quarters of a million and a million people died. Among these people were many young men whose education had begun in the mission schools. Others were the innocent villagers who were strafed by planes overhead, or were lined up and shot by the soldiers for no reason. Still others died at the hand of their own people, a curious turn war often takes. The tribesmen who had left their villages to fight the northern soldiers on the guerrilla side were always in need of food. There is nowhere to get food in the south except from the villagers themselves. So the guerrilla fighters would come into the village and steal grain and cattle. If there was any opposition, they would kill the people.

Kuac remained in Ethiopia for the duration of the war. He learned Amharic and taught in the school system there. However, his status with the church changed when he took a second wife. He wrote me about the problem but made no explanation why he had done what he did. Of course, to him, the marriage was valid; the question imposed and subsequently answered was, Was it sin? The church said it was.

I had a letter from him following his dismissal, in 1968, in which he says:

> I am praying and praising God through Christ as before, and now do not feel sorry for me in thinking of the doubt that perhaps I turned away from the Lord.

He then goes on to speak of his attitude toward himself.

> There is a church building here (in Ethiopia), and a good number of believers worshipping in it. I go on Sundays to worship God with them. They strongly ask me to preach to them the words of God, but I could not help them this time. I needed to be cleansed first by the Savior from all my sins and be free, so I would serve Him again if He still needs me. You, Nyarial, may advise me if I am wrong in this please. I do now help in explaining to them the meaning of the Bible stories and I am still telling them the words of God privately. Is it enough? What do you think? Never mind—the Lord will better tell me what He wants me to do.

In 1972 the Ethiopian government played a major part in reconciling the north and south Sudan, Since that year the fighting has stopped. The south now rules itself under the northern government. The refugees have returned to their land, and Kuac has gone back to Nasir. From there he writes that Man Nyagony, the woman who had said to me, "We will not see your eyes again," has died. Many of the others whom I knew remain.

But a change has come, at least for the moment, brought about by the advantages of the outside world. While in refugee camps the Nuers were given a living stipend for food and clothing. Kuac says in a letter of November 1973 in English,

> The return of the refugees to Sudan brings a great change in culture. Many young people, both men and women, are given jobs and own little money, so they like to have good clothes and fine dresses. Most people in Nasir now understand that they are *turuk* (i.e. a foreigner) and are bound

to wear clothes and hate to walk naked. The old men and women, though, still do not mind much to remain naked, but appreciate and encourage young people to wear clothes.

It remains to be seen how this enforced charity will affect the attitude of the tribe. Contained in this situation is an economic problem not easily solved. But what of the church? Of the people at Nasir, Kuac writes,

> The Lord, Jesus, I have seen is working among the people very well, but their teaching in the ways of Christianity is still small. I pray that God will come and teach me His ways, and make me a good Christian in action, so that I can be able to teach others well, and to teach some of them to be good teachers also of God's Word.

> The way that the Word goes out to many places today is easier than when the missionaries were here. Then the Christians thought the evangelists, who were paid, were like the servants of pastors and missionaries. But now it is clear to every Christian that he is responsible for witnessing for Christ, who is Savior and Lord, and he must witness to his people without money from the church.

Kuac goes on to explain that a great many people come now to the church at Nasir, which meets in the old storeroom there, and to various centers in the surrounding villages as well. But what is occurring in the hearts of the people as genuine faith will be proved only over a long period of time. But a shaken people are at least joining together, and by doing so are hearing the Gospel. For the moment there is no other voice in this lonely land vying for attention. Only God in His sovereignty knows how many will acknowledge and follow Him.

No missionaries are yet permitted to preach in the south Sudan. However, builders, nurses, teachers and doctors have returned and are attempting to build and to plant following the catastrophic war. Mainly their work is in the far south along the southern border, although work is also being done in Malakal, in the Upper Nile Province on the Nile River.

There is no substitute for the cross in the Gospel, neither is there a substitute for the cross in the life of a Christian. Confusion, tears, and heartache follow all men, but for the man or woman who will walk with mankind, bearing the heartache in Christ's name, for that person there is a place in the south Sudan.

The questions remain. Who can drink the cup? Who will follow Him?

Eleanor Vandevort
Gordon College
June 1974

Kuac Nyoat in Nasir (around 1955)

AFTERWORD

The epilogue you have just read was not contained in the original book. It was found among Van's papers in September 2017, just before this 50th anniversary edition went to press. I do not know what prompted her to write it in 1974, almost six years after the publication of *A Leopard Tamed*, but it is a reminder that no story is ever truly complete, that at any moment more of the story may be revealed, that a perceived ending might yet be changed.

This proved to be true in the Sudan. When Van wrote this epilogue, war had passed and the country was being rebuilt. But that was not the end. War came again—and again—and there was more killing and more destruction. Yet there was also something new: immigration to the United States. With that immigration came what can only be viewed in my mind as a providential confluence of events that brought a most unexpected turn to this story.

The full account can be found in Jeff Barker's book *Sioux Center Sudan: A Farm Girl's Missionary Journey* (Hendrickson, 2018). Here, it is enough to say that in all of the killing and despair of the Sudan, a remnant from the village of Nasir survived and found their way to the United States, to Nebraska, to the mission nurse Arlene Schuiteman, and finally to Van. Sarah, Kuac's daughter, was among them. She brought a word of greeting from her father, who was still alive in the Sudan at the time—with whom Van would eventually speak by phone. Although Van was never sentimental and rarely emotional, this turn of events astonished her. Thirty-five years had passed. Continents had been crossed. She had declared her belief many years before that God would be faithful. She had not claimed to know how the fact would show itself.

Photo taken Sunday, April 30, 2006, at First Reformed Church in Sioux Center, Iowa. Kneeling in front: Sarah Kuac (Kuac's daughter). Sitting (from left to right): Dr. Bob Gordon, Eleanor Vandevort, Arlene Schuiteman, Sudanese student, and Man Juba.

It was sometime around 2008 when Van received the news that Kuac had died. She was living with me then, so I remember the call. Van had recounted to me once what Kuac had said as she was preparing to leave the Sudan: "Nyarial, you must write to me. I need to learn many more things." That day, when she learned that Kuac was with the Lord, she hung up the phone and remained quiet for a long time. When she broke her silence, she simply said, "Now it is Kuac who knows everything."

Trudy Summers
Gordon College
October 2017